"We need more believers capable of dividing the human from the divine. Loren Sandford's *Understanding Prophetic People* is a milestone on the road to finding not only those who live in God's presence but those in whom God's presence resides."

—from the foreword by **John Paul Jackson**, founder, Streams Ministries International

"With piercing accuracy, Loren Sandford paints a vivid picture for us in his new book, *Understanding Prophetic People*. Not only will this book grant sanity to prophetically gifted people, but it will also give a measure of peace to pastors in their quest to relate to strongly gifted prophets. This is a welcome addition to the growing arsenal of equipping materials to help mature the prophetic movement."

—**Dr. James W. Goll**, Encounters Network; author, *The Coming Prophetic Revolution, The Seer, Dream Language* and many others

"In *Understanding Prophetic People*, Loren writes from the unique position of being an established prophet himself, but one whose heart is fully and constantly pastoral. Loren continuously asks the questions 'Yes, but what does this mean on the street?' and 'How does this affect the local church?' and 'How will what you say affect the common Christian in the pew each Sunday?' Those questions provide a much-needed check on the prophetic stream. Many emerging prophets have not understood the need for such relevance. Loren makes it clear that each prophet's heart needs to be informed and checked by such questions, and that pastors and church leaders need to understand and minister to the prophetic. Best, he tells us wisdom for the doing. This book ought to be a required manual for both churches and the emerging prophets within them."

—**John Loren Sandford**, co-founder, Elijah House Ministries; author, *The Elijah Task*, *Elijah Among Us* and many others

"When Loren asked me to consider writing an endorsement for his new book, *Understanding Prophetic People*, I looked forward to reading the manuscript, as I have enjoyed and appreciated his previous books. What I was not expecting was a classic! When I first began in prophetic ministry in the early 1980s, Loren's father's book *The Elijah Task* was the classic that I and many others looked to in understanding the ministry of a prophet. What has been sorely missing, however—until now!—was the companion book on the making and makeup of a true prophet. Because the messenger is the message and the prophet is the prophecy, this book is a must-read for both the Church at large and all called by God to be His prophetic spokespeople. It is with real excitement that I recommend the study of this book. It will prove an invaluable, lifelong tool to many who desire to know God's voice and ways."

—**Marc A. Dupont**, Mantle of Praise Ministries, Inc.

UNDERSTANDING
PROPHETIC
PEOPLE

Blessings and Problems
with the Prophetic Gift

R. LOREN SANDFORD

Chosen
Grand Rapids, Michigan

Published by Chosen Books
A division of Baker Publishing Group
P.O. Box 6287, Grand Rapids, MI 49516-6287
www.chosenbooks.com

Printed in the United States of America

Library of Congress Cataloging-in-Publication Data
Sandford, R. Loren.
Understanding prophetic people : blessings and problems with the pro-
phetic gift / R. Loren Sandford.
    p.   cm.
  ISBN 10: 0-8007-9422-2
  ISBN 978-0-8007-9422-4 (pbk.)
  1. Prophecy—Christianity. 2. Gifts, Spiritual. I. Title.
BT767.3.S26 2007
2234'.13—dc22   2007000167

Scripture is taken from the New American Standard Bible®, Copyright © 1960,
1962, 1963, 1968, 1971, 1972, 1973, 1975, 1977, 1995 by The Lockman Foundation. Used by permission.

Excerpt on p. 199 from *Final Steps in Christian Maturity* by Jeanne Guyon and
published by SeedSowers, Jacksonville, FL. Used by permission.

10   11   12   13   14   15   16   10 9 8 7 6 5 4

When I teach on the necessity of the dark night of the soul in the training of a prophet, I often say that my own experience of it lasted twenty years. My loving wife, Beth, always grins at me from the front row and mouths, "Twenty-seven!" It therefore seems only fair to dedicate this book to her. Her loving and gentle support through all that difficult time is one reason I survived to tell about it.

CONTENTS

Foreword

I have been reading and collecting books on or about prophetic ministry for nearly thirty years. In my quest to understand both current and historic views of prophetic ministry, I have perused antique bookstores from New York City to Los Angeles, England to India, and Germany to South Africa. As a result of this search, I have collected old and rare books on this topic, as well as books written by contemporaries. In the process I have come across some remarkable insights and have read far too many horrific statements written by the supposed experts of the time. Even today's writings on prophetic ministry contain, all too often, more foam than substance. So it is a welcome relief to read Loren Sandford's *Understanding Prophetic People*.

This is not a platitude because I like the man!

For years I have wanted to read a book that fairly addresses the issue of prophetic immaturity contrasted with maturity and the current acceptance of prophetic ministry in the Church. In this present era of Church culture, it is important to know what we should expect from prophetic individuals, as well as what those individuals should expect from the Church.

It is also important to understand what I call the "molting process" prophetic individuals go through. Every immature eagle undergoes molting as it transitions from eaglet to adult. During this transition the eaglet loses its soft feathers to grow stronger, longer and more resilient plumage. These new feathers allow the young eagle to soar to heights sometimes two or more miles above the earth. While the soft feathers are falling off, however, the eagle is grounded and defenseless. Here in this dark night of the soul, many prophetic voices lose the battle and are picked off by sinister forces. I am pleased that Loren has taken courage to write clearly on these topics and more.

I am further delighted that he has raised the standard for prophetic ministry. I have long felt that in an effort to recognize her many revelatory individuals, the Church has lowered the bar. In doing so she has inadvertently devalued the preciousness of the Holy Spirit's various gifts and made everyone who has had a dream or acted strangely a prophet of the Most High.

The prophets of Scripture were some of the most disturbing people who have ever lived. Not that they themselves were disturbed, but they did disturb the status quo. In the Church today, too many immature voices think the mark of being prophetic is to act strangely. They even work at it. But being strange no more makes one a prophet than sitting in a garage makes one a car. If a person is prophetic, strange things will happen without his or her trying to manufacture them. Prophetic people, even if they try not to be strange, will experience strange events that few will understand. With great skill, Loren helps us wade through this Catch-22.

I believe the biblical prophet's overriding task was to convey the view of the divine to humanity. That view summed up God's will, His purpose and whatever would keep His creatures from fulfilling what they were created to accomplish, both nationally and individually. For prophets to do this, they had to dismiss their own points of view, their own pain and their own life circumstances in order to speak the oracles of God.

We need more believers capable of dividing the human from the divine. Loren Sandford's *Understanding Prophetic People* is a milestone on the road to finding those who not only live in God's presence but in whom God's presence resides.

John Paul Jackson, founder,
Streams Ministries International

INTRODUCTION

For many years now I have used computers to facilitate various aspects of my ministry. One way to prolong the useful life of an aging PC is to add accelerator chips or memory. The problem with some of these additions is that, while they accelerate the computer and seem to make it more effective or more powerful, they tend to cause problems commensurate with the benefits they bestow. The system freezes. Programs crash and lose valuable data. Eventually you give up, discard the old unit and move to a new, more modern system.

The Church has been doing virtually the same thing with various ministries for many years. We continually add spiritual "technologies"—extrabiblical ideas and teachings intended to enhance ministries and increase manifestations of the power of the Lord. Whether we want to admit it or not, we do it because we have insufficient faith to believe that the simplicity of the revelation delivered to the saints and recorded in Scripture really works. As we begin to employ these spiritual additions and enhancements, the flow of power may at first increase as intended, but ultimately the system begins to crash and we find ourselves losing the very thing we set out to gain.

I believe in the power of the simplicity of the original revelation. In the pages that follow, in addition to addressing issues of major importance, I will pick at things that may seem minor or inconsequential to some of us—mere seeds. But the problem with seeds is that although they start small, they grow into trees. A sprout becomes a trunk, and a trunk grows limbs. Limbs grow leaves. Before long, what seemed to be so small has become something large and destructive—a foreign element incompatible with the essential structure of our precious faith. At that point people get hurt, and wonderful movements of God come to an end while the critics cry, "We told you so!"

In the name of purity I will therefore raise issues and strain out assumptions and practices that I believe to be unbiblical and/or unbalanced, although they may seem to be minor in their significance. True wisdom and true power lie in childlike faith. The less "baggage" the better! If this applies to any average believer, then how much more does it apply to the prophetic person who must live and move in unhindered intimacy with our Lord? Let us seek deeper understanding and wisdom with regard to some issues of foundational significance for prophetic people.

> "Son of man, prophesy against the prophets of Israel who prophesy, and say to those who prophesy from their own inspiration, 'Listen to the word of the LORD! Thus says the Lord GOD, "Woe to the foolish prophets who are follow-ing their own spirit and have seen nothing. O Israel, your prophets have been like foxes among ruins. You have not gone up into the breaches, nor did you build the wall around the house of Israel to stand in the battle on the day of the LORD.

They see falsehood and lying divination who are saying, 'The LORD declares,' when the LORD has not sent them; yet they hope for the fulfillment of their word. Did you not see a false vision and speak a lying divination when you said, 'The LORD declares,' but it is not I who have spoken?'" "Therefore, thus says the Lord GOD, "Because you have spoken falsehood and seen a lie, therefore behold, I am against you," declares the Lord GOD. "So My hand will be against the prophets who see false visions and utter lying divinations. They will have no place in the council of My people, nor will they be written down in the register of the house of Israel, nor will they enter the land of Israel, that you may know that I am the Lord GOD. It is definitely because they have misled My people by saying, 'Peace!' when there is no peace."

Ezekiel 13:2–10

Let us be those who build the walls and fill the breaches for the sake of the Lord's beloved. Let us earn the right to stand in the counsel of the Lord's people. Let us see true visions and practice not divination but genuine intimacy with God.

PART 1

FOUNDATIONS

1

A PROFILE OF THE PROPHETIC PERSON

Prophetic people are generally weird. I can say it no other way. Who among those in the charismatic wing of the Church has not found at least some prophetic people to be "a few French fries short of a Happy Meal," as a friend of mine puts it? They can be wonderful, but they can also come across as confusing, extreme, crusty, unbalanced, defensive and moody.

Church leaders often have difficulty working with prophetic people, possessing little clue how to pastor this kind of gift and personality. Lay people are either disproportionately attracted to them for their supposed spirituality and its potential benefit to them or repelled for reasons they scarcely understand. Real acceptance can be a rare and lovely experience.

These people—these precious ones with such potential to hear from God for the edification of the Church—require understanding and nurture in the same way and for the same reasons others do. But the Church often fails them. She sometimes even abuses and wounds them through lack of understanding of who they are and what kinds of influences have shaped them.

To be fair, prophetic people often have earned the stripes the Body of Christ inflicts upon them. They are as needy as anyone else, neither more holy nor more spiritual than those who do not share the prophetic gift.

But we prophets have been configured a little differently because of our particular calling. The apostle Paul wrote, "We have gifts that differ according to the grace given to us" (Romans 12:6). Not better—just different!

What kind of person is prophetic? Is there a personality profile that accompanies the gift? Are there life experiences common to prophetic people that result in similar defining characteristics?

Prophetic people vary in nature as widely as the population in general, while sharing to a significant degree a number of personality elements and life experiences. We come in all sizes and shapes, some of us serious in nature and some of us loving a good joke, some intellectual and others having no education at all. But at heart, we are much alike in many respects.

I would like to begin by sharing some characteristics common to prophetic people. In so doing, I hope to help the Church to better recognize, equip and reach out to people blessed with this gift. And to prophetic people, I say, "You are not alone!"

Rarely Happy

Rarely are prophetic people "happy" people—at least until they have served long and made peace with the gift, with the pain of the burden it brings and with God. For a prophetic person, training involves depths of crushing and breaking that seem incomprehensible to the average Christian. Later chapters will deal with the shape of this wilderness experience, but for now understand that the training period and the heaviness of spirit that may accompany it can last for many years.

This heaviness need not be permanent. Seasoned prophetic people who have persevered over time in seeking the presence and heart of God and have allowed suffering to effect the character changes it was intended to produce come at last into a deep abiding peace and joy that are not easily shaken. One source of the dark moodiness that so plagues some prophetic types, therefore, is the pressure of the constant seasons of crucifixion required to produce the character adjustments that are so essential to the calling.

Burden Bearing

Burden bearing is one of the most difficult aspects of prophetic awareness to sort out and balance. Galatians 6:2, "Bear one another's burdens, and thereby fulfill the law of Christ," expresses both a command and an awareness felt acutely by every prophetic person I know.

Not all burden bearers are prophetic, but all prophetic people are burden bearers. We deeply feel everything going on in the hearts of people around us. Some of us feel it for the nation and the world. Some bear the burden for a region or local church. Others carry the hearts of other people one at a time. Some even bear the heart of God in such a way. We carry it in our own hearts as if it were our own.

The lives of biblical prophets illustrate this bearing of burdens. The emotional weight of the faithlessness and unrighteousness of Israel so crushed Moses that he pled with God to kill him (see Numbers 11:15). Jeremiah bore the burden of Israel's sin and the coming destruction so deeply that scholars have dubbed him "the weeping prophet."

I recall visiting my girlfriend's home on the top of a mountain overlooking Spokane, Washington, when I was just sixteen years old. From the huge picture window in the living room, the entire city stretched out below like a sparkling jewel glittering in the night. As I stood before that window one evening gazing out at the lights, an almost physical force of something I did not understand came rushing up at me from the city and flooded my heart. I began to weep without an inkling of understanding why. I knew only that the grief overwhelmed me. Years later I understood that my Lord had identified my heart and spirit with the sin and pain of the people and had allowed me to feel it compassionately, to bear the burden of it within myself for a moment.

Had I understood it at the time, I would have answered the call to pray, but I was too young. Prophetic analysis and understanding of that kind of prompting came later. Instead, at the age of sixteen it became part of my ongoing struggle with depression and added to my sense of weirdness, not to mention the judgment of others that I was a bit strange.

Most prophetic people I know today are much like I was at that early age. They lack the awareness, training and seasoning necessary to sort out what emotional currents are theirs personally from those that are not, and they cannot avoid being overwhelmed. After a lifetime of working with it, this remains a battle for me—a battle I sometimes lose. Without good pastoring or coaching from others who understand and whose differing gifts balance those of the prophetic person, depressive burden-bearing episodes can become a prison of habit that enforces isolation from real connection with others. So the budding prophet gets labeled as weird and/or unstable.

In my early years of ministry as an adult, I would force myself to think it through: *Is there any reason in my own life for me to be feeling these things?* If an adequate answer could not be found in my own situation, I would assume that the things I was feeling had their source in something I was sensing for someone else. When I had determined that it came from somewhere outside myself, I would pray for revelation, to know whether it originated in an individual or in some wider issue affecting groups of people or nations. Finally, I would pray concerning whatever revelation I received. Even today I begin that way when the burdens come.

The trouble began when my childhood training took over. From my earliest years I was schooled in emotional control and suppression rather than healthy emotional release. Consequently I would identify certain feelings as coming from an outside source and then put them in another "room" in my heart without dealing with them while I went on about my daily business. It was a form of suppression that felt natural and right to me because of the way I had been trained.

Not until years later did I learn how destructive that approach was. In that other room, the feelings had nowhere to go. Much like a septic tank that eventually needs to be pumped in order to remain functional, the feelings only built up and became infected until I was overcome by a huge mass of undefined pain and confusion that could no longer be controlled or understood. The room had been filled until I could put nothing more in it. The pain I had locked away in that place began to overflow, and it became ever more difficult for me to hear God clearly or to see any of the positive things He was accomplishing in my life and ministry.

I fell into clinical depression and remained there for many years, although I continued to function as a pastor, husband and father. Several attempts at counseling led nowhere, having run aground on the failure of my counselors to understand what they were dealing with, not to mention my own blockheaded rigidity.

At last, at the perfect time in my life and in the plan of God, I met a healing couple whose tools and level of compassion were just the right stuff. With their help God granted release and freedom, not just in the area of burden bearing, but in my entire emotional life. Everyone connected with me benefited, beginning with my family. Prophetically gifted people need differently gifted people for balance, healing and wholeness.

Months after that wonderful release, I found myself once again overwhelmed. Waves of paranoia, fear and despair that I knew had no root in my own life threatened to sweep me away, but this time the outcome was different. Good counseling had at last connected me with the Father's love at a level I had never before known, so that as I sought the Lord in prayer, He did something new with me. I share it here as a symbolic visual representation of the scriptural command in 1 Peter 5:6–7: "Therefore humble yourselves under the mighty hand of God, that He may exalt you at the proper time, *casting all your anxiety on Him, because He cares for you*" (emphasis mine).

As I prayed, I suddenly felt as if I were standing under and inside the mouth of a tornado of the Holy Spirit swirling all around me. This inverted funnel served as a great vortex drawing paranoia, fear and despair out of the people of my church and up through me to the Lord.

After what must have been about thirty minutes of this form of resting in the Spirit and letting the swirling funnel do its work, I fell into a state of perfect peace. Better than this, I was filled with a clean, rested and holy love for the people of my church that I had not felt in a long time. That day, as I participated in a *quinceañera* (a fifteenth-year rite of passage for a girl in Mexican culture) for one of the families in our church, I enjoyed a whole new sense of tender love and joy for my people as I moved among them.

Today I take care to remember the inverted funnel and what it means for passing things through to Jesus. It helps keep me in the Lord's joy and prevents my spiritual plumbing from clogging up with unsurrendered burdens picked up from the people around me. Jesus is the burden bearer/intercessor—not me. I am just a servant. Burden bearing can be a prophetic indicator pointing the way to prayer, but done wrongly, it can be enormously destructive. Dealing with burden bearing can be one of the most difficult learning curves for any prophetic person to master, and it can feed a state of persistent unhappiness.

The Gift of Weakness

I have already mentioned the necessity of the wilderness in the life of the prophetic person. Even with the abiding peace and joy that come with maturity, some elements of wilderness suffering never end, starting with the gift of weakness.

Because of the surpassing greatness of the revelations, for this reason, to keep me from exalting myself, there was given me a thorn in the flesh, a messenger of Satan to torment me—to keep me from exalting myself! Concerning this I implored the Lord three times that it might leave me. And He has said to me, "My grace is sufficient for you, for power is perfected in weakness." Most gladly, therefore, I will rather boast about my weaknesses, so that the power of Christ may dwell in me. Therefore I am well content with weaknesses, with insults, with distresses, with persecutions, with difficulties, for Christ's sake; for when I am weak, then I am strong.

2 Corinthians 12:7–10

Paul pled three times for release from his thorn in the flesh but was denied for his own sake and that of the Kingdom of God (see 2 Corinthians 12). The flesh remains a persistent and relentless opponent requiring much discipline from the Father who loves us.

"Then Jesus said to His disciples, 'If anyone wishes to come after Me, he must deny himself, and take up his cross and follow Me'" (Matthew 16:24). Luke 9:23 adds the word *daily*. What is the cross if not an instrument of death? Is it not the place where corrupt flesh dies so that new life can emerge in union with Jesus in His resurrection?

While every believer responding to the call to discipleship must live this life of the cross, it must go deeper for the prophetic person, and so there are constant blows to pride and ego and to those elements of character that do not yet resonate the character of Jesus. Sometimes this aspect of the heavy hand of God sends me into seasons of heaviness, but mostly at this stage of my life I can welcome it in gratitude and go on with joy undisturbed. "A rebuke goes deeper into one who has understanding than a hundred blows into a fool" (Proverbs 17:10). "Faithful are the wounds of a friend, but deceitful are the kisses of an enemy" (Proverbs 27:6). And what a friend I have in Jesus!

But this life of humbling and breaking can cause the prophetic person, especially the immature and unseasoned one, to appear to be constantly unhappy.

Eccentric Personalities

Prophetic types are usually eccentric personalities who have experienced more than their share of rejection because they do not think, feel or even act like other people. Not only are they misunderstood by others—even by their families and intimate loved ones—but they are seldom understood even by themselves. Like so many things prophetic people face internally, this lack of self-understanding diminishes with maturity and healing, but I do not know of a prophetic person who has not experienced it.

Self-Protections

Many a burden-bearing child with prophetic gifts becomes the family scapegoat, the repository of everything other family members cannot face or express. Instinctively, brothers and sisters—and parents, as well—project their pain onto the moody one, often acting it out with ridicule and torment until a root of rejection takes hold that shapes life and pollutes perceptions.

Additionally, the prophetic child may experience things that seem strange or weird to others: dreams, visitations in the night by angels or demons, visions and things the prophetic child can "see" that others cannot. He or she may innocently share these things with the rest of the family and be ridiculed for it, which serves only to reinforce a growing root of rejection and a sense of imminent danger everywhere in the child's world.

In response, such a child may develop illegal self-protections based in judgments on others and fear of vulnerability that carry over into adult life. As a result, the prophetic person may subconsciously and sometimes deliberately reject the very fellowship that would be so healing and helpful if only he or she were able to enter into it.

Worse, these self-protective judgments and fears can open the door to demonic influences masquerading as God. Genuine prophetic gifts can be invaded and co-opted for the enemy's unclean purposes while the victim never knows the difference. If not faced head-on, this can lead to compromised ministry in which perceptions and words become demonically inspired and destructive in ways that become obvious to everyone but the one giving them. Such demonic influence can turn the gift of discernment into something invasive and violating to others. Thus compromised, the prophetic person may see into things a demon reveals but that God would have concealed. He or she may demand vulnerability of others without ever sharing anything of real substance from his or her own heart. The information gained may then be used to strengthen his or her own sphere of influence and sense of position at the expense of those who should have been receiving ministry. All this begins with sinful self-protection. People instinctively react to this with mistrust, which adds to the problem of rejection.

Loneliness and Isolation

As eccentrics, we prophetic people ask questions about life and faith that do not seem to matter to others and, in pondering these questions, we often find ourselves off in a dream world somewhere while the rest of the world passes us by. We look for answers in places others never seem to consider, and we seek the deep meaning of things others seem to accept at face value. We find ourselves incapable of settling for anything that strikes us as shallow. The quest often consumes so much of our awareness that we seem disconnected, even aloof, from other people. Life seems to hold a different set of meanings for us.

Because of this lack of common perspective, people sometimes have trouble relating to us as friends and peers, while we, in turn, have trouble relating to them. For instance, when all that matters to me is the spiritual significance of the next natural disaster, it can become difficult to join others in their excitement over last Sunday's victory for the local professional football team, when in truth I would be healthier and a more balanced human being if I could join others in their excitement.

Being prophetic can bring imbalance and enforce a profound sense of loneliness and isolation. Normal folk do not know how to relate to us, and we do not know how to relate to them.

Prophetic people live as forerunners. They are usually one step ahead of the rest of the Body of Christ. When other people are down and out, the prophetic person may already be rejoicing in the blessing to come. Or when others catch up and find the joy and blessing the prophet saw coming, the prophet has already moved on and now grieves over the failure and apostasy that will form the essence of the coming days.

In my own ministry, I have always seemed to be on a different page than everyone else. For instance, I am a worship leader, but God has never allowed me to do the music everyone else is doing. I am always different, always writing in a different vein or choosing different songs from the mainstream—not better, just different, but often different in directions and ways the rest of the Body will walk in later.

When the Father's love became the major emphasis in my wing of the renewal movement, it brought healing, refreshment and hope to untold thousands, and I supported it 100 percent. But prophetically I sensed an imbalance. I knew that if we focused on the Father's love at the expense of an emphasis on the cross and the blood, we would suffer loss for the imbalance. From the beginning I spoke for the corrective balance, sometimes moving against the mainstream in doing so. Not until years later at a high-level meeting of the leadership of our movement did the top officers confess that we had focused on the Father's love at the expense of the centrality of Jesus and His sacrifice. A time of repentance followed. I found that many others had longed for that day as I had, and shared the same concerns, but for years I felt out of step with the mainstream.

This loneliness and isolation can cause damage to more than ministry. It is not unusual to find significant conflict in a prophetic marriage because the prophetic one is so often not "present" for the mate. This is, of course, a sinful dysfunction—a form of self-absorption—but these things can take time to overcome. Worse, until the root of rejection is healed, the prophetic person can misinterpret even innocent things his or her mate does. Something as simple as a call to "Come out of it!" can be interpreted as criticism and rejection. We are as broken and wounded as anyone else—and often more so.

I left home in 1969, but I can still see my father sunk down in his easy chair, lost in a world of his own, pondering the deep mysteries of the universe while my mother stood defiantly before him, hands planted firmly on her hips, fire leaping from her eyes as she nearly shouted, "John! You come out here and talk with me!" After several minutes of this, he would suddenly look up at her as if nothing had been going on and grunt, "Huh?" Of course, by this time she was furious, while he acted as though his feelings were hurt, bewildered as to why she would be so upset.

The same thing would happen as we children tore up the house and fought with one another. Mom would call for help while Dad remained oblivious and withdrawn, plumbing the depths of some question of profound spiritual significance. Eventually my desperate mother would lose her temper in her demands that he be aware and helpful. It was not easy for either of them. Obviously being married to a prophetic person can require extra measures of both patience and understanding, especially when the wounds of rejection in the prophetic person go back to childhood and color present perceptions of every relationship.

Uncommon Experiences

In this memory I am perhaps six years old. It is 3:00 A.M., and I have been awakened by a breeze of wonderful power-filled wind and light blowing the full length of my body and causing me to feel as if I am floating a foot above my bed. I have no idea what this is, but I know it is wonderful! As I reach out to take hold of it to try to make it last, it fades away as if the window through which it came were slowly being closed.

In another memory I am awakened during the night at about the same time by a smothering force that paralyzes and terrifies me. This time I struggle, and when I can finally speak, I cry out, "Dad!" He comes running to my bedside to hold and comfort me. When at last I feel quiet and secure, he explains that I have been attacked by an evil spirit and that when it happens again I must use the name of Jesus. This was my first practical lesson in Philippians 2:10: "So that at the name of Jesus every knee will bow, of those who are in heaven and on earth and under the earth." I tearfully inform my father that when I am attacked, I cannot speak, but he assures me that the demon will know what I am trying to say. I tested his instruction the next time I experienced a similar attack and found that he was absolutely right.

I thought everyone had these experiences. I really believed that all fathers paid visits to the heavens during the night and had dreams shared by their friends thousands of miles away in which they met with one another and conversed. How painful it was to be ridiculed and even ostracized by other children when I innocently shared these things!

What other sixteen-year-old stands in his girlfriend's living room weeping over the city for no discernable reason? What do his testosterone-driven friends—which describes any and all sixteen-year-old boys, including the prophetic ones—think of such things? What can a kid who ponders the depth of every question and who settles for no easy answers find in common with those whose lives consist of sports, fighting, girls and beer? Sometimes he tries joining them in these things, but he suffers profoundly for it.

Another teenager with a prophetic destiny walks into an empty room at night and stops dead in his tracks, adrenaline suddenly driving his heart rate higher as a vision of a medieval warrior in full armor and weaponry appears below a canopy of swirling demons. He chokes down an urge to cry out audibly in the name of Jesus and reaches for the light switch to make it all go away as his friends file through the door behind him. Warfare in the heavenlies comes early to this young and frightened prophet.

Even in his teens the prophet must avert his eyes from directly engaging others because they can seem so penetrating that his gaze makes them uncomfortable. Girlfriends do not last long because his emotional intensity burns them out, while his discernment lets him see more of their hurt and confusion than they are comfortable with.

At seventeen a young prophet attends a bachelor party where friends of the groom had hired a stripper. He is the only virgin in the room, and so the stripper singles him out for a lap dance. As she plants herself in his face, his only defense against this unwelcome invasion is to prophesy her life story to her. Deeply shaken, she backs away and leaves the party.

The young prophet walks alone, even when he is with others—and then only if he can learn to play their games and find their rhythms. Or he leads the pack, creating the flow himself without really becoming one of the gang because at heart he is relationally dysfunctional. He may never have a truly close friend. He learned long ago not to share what he really sees and feels. If he is blessed, he may find a mate whose special qualities of patience and kindness equip her to carry his heart. Again, he needs the balance, love and correction of those who walk in other gifts.

How he deals with loneliness will determine the shape of his life, whether it becomes a hard walk of bitterness in isolation and self-protection or a place of deep, sweet and private communion with God that becomes a fountainhead of peace and love for the sake of others. He may vacillate between the two extremes until he settles on one side or the other. With good help and the hand of God he will make the right choices. Without that help he may join the ranks of those unsubmitted, bitter and arrogant pseudo-spiritual, self-appointed so-called prophets who torment pastors and their congregations with streams of condemnation and judgment—until they are asked to leave. He may become a Jezebel, using his gifts in illegal, self-protective ways to build a power base under his control at his pastor's expense and to the detriment of his church.

Awareness Deficits

Prophetic personalities often have little consciousness of what might be viewed by others as weird behavior, and they may tend to communicate in ways that neither they nor others fully understand. John the Baptist, for example, wore camel skin and ate bugs. Hardly normal! Ezekiel dug holes in the city wall and carried his travel baggage around all day just for people to see (see Ezekiel 12). And that was nothing compared to Ezekiel 4, in which he built a toy city in the public place and then lay down by it for the better part of 430 days. If that were not enough, he had himself tied up with ropes. He did all this just to proclaim the siege and destruction of Jerusalem and the deportation of the population into exile. "Normal" people would never entertain such instructions as coming from God.

My prophetic father never seemed to know or care what people might think of his abnormal behavior, whether or not that behavior was supposed to be prophetic. I always knew, for instance, when he was on his way home because I could hear him singing in tongues at the top of his lungs as he walked the several blocks from the church. Never mind that the neighborhood could hear him! Countless Sundays he got himself in hot water with the people of the church for preaching his latest prophetic revelation, with little thought as to how it might affect them. I am not sure he cared about that, but I know my mother did, and she let him know it over and over again.

The Fruit of Rejection

The prophet inevitably faces rejection. In Bible times they threw Jeremiah down a well. Elijah fled for his life to escape death at the hands of Jezebel. Listen to Jeremiah, brokenhearted from the rejection he endured at the hands of those he loved and served:

> O LORD, You have deceived me and I was deceived; You have overcome me and prevailed. I have become a laughingstock all day long; everyone mocks me. For each time I speak, I cry aloud; I proclaim violence and destruction, because for me the word of the LORD has resulted in reproach and derision all day long. But if I say, "I will not remember Him or speak anymore in His name," then in my heart it becomes like a burning fire shut up in my bones; and I am weary of holding it in, and I cannot endure it. For I have heard the whispering of many, "Terror on every side! Denounce him; yes, let us denounce him!" All my trusted friends, watching for my fall, say: "Perhaps he will be deceived, so that we may prevail against him and take our revenge on him."
>
> Jeremiah 20:7–10

I have experienced my own share of rejection. During my high school years in the 1960s, we lived in a small mining town. My father pastored a church there just two blocks from the street where five houses of prostitution operated openly under neon signs advertising their presence. My father spoke prophetically against them and drew persecution for it. When I was sixteen years old, I wrote a letter to the editor of the local newspaper in which I spoke against the presence of these houses of ill repute and outlined what other communities thought of our city—and especially of our girls—as a result of their presence. I was a musician in a traveling rock group at the time, and so I knew firsthand what other cities thought of us.

The town rose up in virtual unison to persecute us for challenging this "sacred" institution. Anonymous phone calls were made to our home questioning if I was really a man.

In addition to this, my parents pioneered the charismatic movement in our denomination, as well as inner healing for the wider Body of Christ. Later, I joined them and helped develop the material. We were prophetic forerunners. As a result of this, we suffered persecution on every side. Vile accusations were made. The teachings were twisted and distorted beyond all recognition in order to create justification for vilification.

True prophetic people who have not yet fully made peace with the calling and its consequences can therefore seem hard at times. They can appear to be angry and defensive because they are geared up and armored in advance against the negative responses they expect to receive. They have been lied about, misunderstood and misrepresented—and it hurts. We prophets would like to be as forgiving as Jesus, but we are just like anyone else. We are works in progress, not finished products.

What may therefore seem to be pride can actually be simple defensiveness. What appears to be a hard and arrogant exterior can conceal a gentle and wounded heart of love. Those who would nurture prophetic people must work to see past this defensive—and even offensive—exterior.

My own family has fought a long battle against a pattern of always gearing up for a fight. Worse, we developed a stronghold of arrogant hubris to cover our sense of rejection. The rest of the world—the source of so much pain—was sick, but we were not. We had the revelation. We knew what life was really about. We were the mature ones in possession of the truth because of the experiences we shared. The rest of the Christian world just did not know. We have spent years working to break that stronghold so that our pride and arrogance would not defile others, but the battle never ends. The flesh can be a stubborn enemy!

Those who would minister to prophetic people must take these things into account and determine to see past them. Compassion and understanding, rather than frontal assault on perceived character flaws, wins the day. Trust comes hard to the prophetic person, but the one who comes in love can earn it.

Life-Threatening Events

It is not unusual for a prophetic type—or anyone with a high calling—to have been born in the midst of some kind of life-threatening trauma or to have a history of scrapes with death or serious injury, especially in childhood. The enemy of our soul has an obvious vested interest in cutting off a destiny before it can happen, especially when that destiny touches the lives of many others.

Pharaoh sought to kill all the male babies in Israel in order to reduce the threat their numbers represented. Moses' family saved his life by placing him in a basket and floating him downriver, where Pharaoh's daughter found him and raised him as her own. Jesus was born under similar circumstances. Herod tried desperately to kill Jesus before He could reach the age of two.

I am no Moses and certainly no Jesus, but I bear a calling. When my mother was in labor with me, the hospital fouled up her anesthesia. I could have been stillborn.

My life since birth has been peppered with near misses. One clear example happened on the ski slope. I am an expert skier, but one time I felt myself supernaturally hurled into the air off a ski jump I knew well. I found myself surrounded by blackness and much too high to land safely. I overshot the slope that would have taken up the force of my descent and came down with such an impact that both my skis popped off. The loss of my skis threw me forward onto the top of my head in rock-solid, hard-packed snow, driving my chin into my chest with the force of my 225 pounds and the power of momentum. A ski patrolman who witnessed the accident thought I was dead. I got up and skied away, but my neck hurt for weeks. I later learned that one of the prophetic prayer people in my congregation had been warned in a dream and had prayed for my protection before I went to the mountain.

I have heard similar stories of near misses from many others. Prophetic people need to be covered by protective prayers from those who love them. Lives and destinies are at stake in an ongoing war.

Overserious about Life in General

Prophetic people are often overserious about life and themselves and may have real difficulty just laughing and playing. Some discover their callings late in life, having had no inkling beforehand, but many are born with a crushing sense of destiny. From earliest childhood they live under a sense of urgency.

I cannot remember a time when I did not feel a sense of urgent destiny. As a child I could not wait to grow up. At the age of two I spoke with the clarity and vocabulary of a child twice my age. I did everything early. They called me "the little old man" even before I started school. Once in school I refused to sing "kid" songs because they seemed so silly and immature. The teacher thought I was being unco-operative. I felt there was no time for childhood! I had a destiny to fulfill!

Part of this seriousness comes from the other attributes and influences I have already listed. The prophetic person often feels all these things long before there is any possibility of understanding them. Consequently, the prophet has little time to play freely and not much room to laugh, until maturity, seasoning and the cross bring his or her character to rest.

In middle age, I am just now finding my freedom. Maturity for the prophetic person can take a lot longer than for the one who does not walk under the burden of such a calling. It is the difference between sprinting the one hundred meters and running the marathon. The goal is farther away, and it takes longer to get there.

What the Church Needs to Do

In light of all this, it is obvious that most prophetic people need serious healing work. God has given us the tools to accomplish this through the various streams and forms of Christian counseling that have emerged over the last few decades. Holiness and character transformation at the deepest levels are imperative for the prophetic person. The resources are out there. We have only to avail ourselves of them. And churches need to provide these resources for prophetic people and then encourage them in walking through their healing.

Pastors and leaders must nurture prophetic people with grace and understanding, without taking offense at their quirks and issues of brokenness. It is too easy to be defensive or fearful when these wounded people cross boundaries or act out their fears and lacerations of heart. They may act as though they have a higher calling than others, but they do not. They may assume more authority than is theirs, but correction can be brought. Only let it be brought with compassion and love, and with an eye to healing.

Prophetic people need loving friends to make them play, laugh (especially at themselves) and celebrate the goodness of their humanity. Over the years God has sent me true friends who informed me—they did not ask me—that I was going skiing the following Tuesday. One brother would simply present himself at my front door and inquire with a grin on his face, "Can Loren come out and play?" Outside on his trailer would be a pair of go-carts. Off we would go for a couple of hours of fun! I came back refreshed and more balanced than when I left.

Finally, every church needs people of prayer who take prophetic people into their hearts to be watchmen and watchwomen for their lives. In Ephesians 6:18–20 the apostle Paul wrote:

> With all prayer and petition pray at all times in the Spirit, and with this in view, be on the alert with all perseverance and petition for all the saints, and pray on my behalf, that utterance may be given to me in the opening of my mouth, to make known with boldness the mystery of the gospel, for which I am an ambassador in chains; that in proclaiming it I may speak boldly, as I ought to speak.

In short, Paul called for prayers of protection and prayers for the effectiveness of his ministry. We prophetic people are lost without that kind of support.

2

PROPHETIC MINISTRY

An Overview

I n order to fully understand the heart of the prophetic person we must understand the nature of prophetic calling and ministry. This becomes all the more necessary in light of the current proliferation of confusion in the Body of Christ concerning prophetic issues. In this chapter I will answer some questions regarding prophetic ministry and provide a general overview of it.

Definition of Prophetic Ministry

Prophetic ministry is never primarily prediction, although prediction can be part of it. The Greek word for *prophet* is *prophemi*. It has two parts. *Pro* means "forth." *Phemi* means "to speak." The primary meaning of the word, therefore, is to speak forth for the Lord rather than to predict.

The first definition of the word *prophecy* is found in the Old Testament. It flows from God's explanation to Jeremiah concerning the nature of his calling: "See, I have appointed you this day over the nations and over the kingdoms, to pluck up and to break down, to destroy and to overthrow, to build and to plant" (Jeremiah 1:10). This verse defines the scope of Jeremiah's ministry as a prophet: over nations and kingdoms. It also defines the nature of the prophetic word in any age. The prophetic word tears down what the Lord has not authored while it releases power to plant and to build the purposes of God. Something about the genuine prophetic word kindles things in the hearts of God's servants and releases power to set those things in motion. It tears down false doctrines and obstacles raised up against the purposes of God, and it restores His people to the foundation in Him necessary for the unfolding of His plans and intentions.

This Old Testament understanding of the word forms the basis for the New Testament definition of *prophecy* as stated by the apostle Paul: "But one who prophesies speaks to men for edification and exhortation and consolation" (1 Corinthians 14:3). *Prophetic ministry, then, is words and insights inspired by the Holy Spirit for the edification, consolation and exhortation of the Body of Christ, passed through the filter of the minds and hearts of men and women.*

Genuine prophetic ministry releases power and encouragement for building up the people of God to accomplish His will. Mature prophetic people are consumed with concern for others.

Prophetic Restoration

"It will come about after this that I will pour out My Spirit on all mankind; and your sons and daughters will prophesy, your old men will dream dreams, your young men will see visions. Even on the male and female servants I will pour out My Spirit in those days. I will display wonders in the sky and on the earth, blood, fire and columns of smoke. The sun will be turned into darkness and the moon into blood before the great and awesome day of the LORD comes."

Joel 2:28–31

This Old Testament prophecy has been only partially fulfilled even today. Joel's prophetic word includes unfulfilled elements and a foreshadowing of greater things yet to come.

Some prophetic passages in Scripture see multiple fulfillments in history. Others do not. Sorting out which is which requires that the believer discern whether or not the passage was fulfilled one to one in history, or if it embodied foreshadowing of larger things that have not yet been fulfilled in any way. When we see a one-to-one fulfillment in history without any foreshadowing or pieces yet unfulfilled, we ought not to look for further fulfillments. The prophecy is complete. But when a passage has been only partly fulfilled in history or when it contains foreshadowing of greater things than can be seen in the historical fulfillment, then we must expect other fulfillments to unfold.

On the Day of Pentecost, for instance, the Holy Spirit fell upon the disciples in an unprecedented way (see Acts 2). He manifested physically in a sound like a mighty rushing wind and in tongues of fire that appeared over their heads. The disciples spoke in tongues, and thousands came to Jesus. In his sermon to the gathered crowd that day Peter explained, "This is what was spoken of through the prophet Joel" (Acts 2:16). It was not, however, a complete fulfillment. They saw no wonders in the sky, the moon did not turn to blood, and the sun did not become darkness. The great and terrible end-time Day of the Lord did not come as Joel had prophesied.

43

Pentecost was but one partial fulfillment of a larger and more extensive prophecy. We must therefore expect more than one fulfillment to unfold in history. We understand that one day a full and final fulfillment will include all the elements of Joel's word. Until then, whenever God sends a visitation of the Holy Spirit with end-time intensity, we should expect His voice to be heard by average believers and for relationship with Him to be renewed in a living way.

In addition, we should expect a revival of prophetic ministry. After Pentecost came Agabus and the daughters of Philip, whom Scripture recognizes as prophets. As God poured out His Spirit, the Church experienced a broad revival of the prophetic voice. Paul spoke of prophetic ministry and the proper exercise of it in 1 Corinthians 14. In light of Joel's prophecy and the aftermath of Pentecost, it therefore seems reasonable to expect similar revivals of the prophetic voice to accompany any significant outpouring of the Holy Spirit.

In the current movement of the Holy Spirit, then, it makes sense that we are seeing a corresponding revival of prophetic ministry. As God pours out His Spirit, He is restoring prophetic ministry—with all its warts, wrinkles and, yes, value to the Body of Christ.

A Foundational Ministry

The apostle Paul saw prophets as one of the foundations of the Church. Ephesians 2:20–22 speaks of the Church as a household,

> having been built on the foundation of the apostles and prophets, Christ Jesus Himself being the corner stone, in whom the whole building, being fitted together, is growing into a holy temple in the Lord, in whom you also are being built together into a dwelling of God in the Spirit.

Traditionally we have understood the foundation of the apostles to be the New Testament Scriptures. We have believed prophets in this context to be figures like Isaiah and Jeremiah. The problem with this is that Jesus, the cornerstone, is alive and never wrote a word. Why should we then understand the apostles and prophets to be the writings only of men who have died? And to be consistent, if Jesus is alive, then we must see apostles and prophets as living persons—living apostles who build churches and exercise translocal authority, and living prophets who inform the Body of Christ in a variety of ways. Another way to see it is that apostles are the foremen on the building project while prophets are the building inspectors who make certain the building goes up according to the divine building code. In any case, we need our foundational people.

In this passage Paul painted a picture of an archway with apostles and prophets at the bases of the arch. As living stones, we form the curving walls of the arch, while Jesus as the cornerstone at the apex nevertheless bears the weight of the arches. Everything points upward to Him, and in Him it all holds together. But essential to the structure is a functioning foundational prophetic ministry.

Prophetic ministry restores a measure of integrity, guidance and preparation to the Church. It also restores the foundation God intended.

Prophetic Ministry Prepares God's People for His Purposes

In a world filled with both unprecedented opportunities and towering obstacles, we need *all* our tools. Accurate prophetic ministry has the potential to alert us to opportunities before they open up so we can respond quickly

and effectively. It can reveal to us ways and means to overcome opposition. Churches can be strengthened, missions
expanded, individuals strategically deployed and more. Note
the following examples.

When my wife and I received our call to Denver, the Lord
showed her our home in a vision so that we recognized it
when we saw it. As I struggled with whether or not to leave
our longtime home in northern Idaho, an angel visited me
in a dream and not only affirmed the move to Denver but
also showed me in symbolism what would happen in the
first few years there. A leading prophet with a national voice
called to tell me, "You are being sent to Denver," and went
on to define the specific purpose for which we were being
sent. The prophetic word was instrumental in placing us
where the Lord wanted us to be and helped prepare us for
the obstacles we would face.

Before the onset of the disastrous and record-setting 2005
hurricane season, the Lord showed me—and a number of
others around the country—the devastation that would
come to Florida and the Gulf Coast. We called for prayer.
As Hurricane Rita closed in on the Texas coast, our local
prayer people were holding our regular Thursday prayer
meeting at the church. The Lord told me to cry out for
mercy, that there was still time to mitigate the impact of
that powerful storm, even with only twelve hours to go.
I "saw" in a mental vision the hand of God close over the
hurricane and begin to squeeze. We prayed. Over the next
few hours Rita shrank from a category four to a category
three. It then angled just enough to the east to miss the
major population centers and spare the heart of our nation's
oil-refining capacity. I am certain we were not alone and
that many others were praying the same thing. I am equally
certain that the intercession of these saints, much of it in-

spired prophetically, moved the heart of God to mitigate the impact of that hurricane.

In 1997 a prophetic ministry team in Toronto prophesied that my son would "shake the world" (their language, not ours) in youth ministry. At that time my wife and I were deeply concerned about his spiritual state and worried that he might not respond to his calling. A year later he chose to take the helm of our youth group and continue his education at Denver Seminary after completing his BA in psychology. Today our youth group is one of the largest in the Denver metro area, complete with revival manifestations of every kind. That prophetic word helped prepare us to prepare him for the ministry God had reserved for him.

Years before the Toronto Blessing broke out in 1994, prophetic voices spoke of what would happen there. The outpouring in Toronto has dramatically affected the progress of the Gospel worldwide in ways that can scarcely be calculated and will not be understood fully for many years to come.

Prophetic words helped set in motion the events that produced the Promise Keepers movement in the 1990s that has had such a profound impact on men around the world. Promise Keepers continues its work today, touching many thousands of lives for Jesus.

Similar things have happened in numerous other places. Such words of promise serve to prepare the Body of Christ to carry out His will and to receive what God intends to send.

Prophetic Dangers

As we consider the many benefits of prophetic ministry to the Body of Christ, it is important to understand that merely because someone heard from God does not necessarily make the hearer prophetic. Hearing from God is the birthright of every Christian in a living relationship with our Father and Lord. All of us should hear from Him devotionally and personally. Very little, if any, of what we hear is for public consumption or prophetic in any sense of the word. A word becomes prophetic only when it carries authority to affect the purposes of God in the individual lives of others, the Church and the world. Part of maturing in prophetic ministry is therefore learning to differentiate what is truly prophetic from what is merely personal. This requires a second level of listening. The prophet must pray, "All right, Lord, I heard from You. Now what do You want me to do with what I have heard?"

In addition, the Church must be careful with prophetic words! I cannot say this strongly enough. Many of the world's cults have begun with a supposed prophetic word. For instance, the Mormon Church, with all its doctrinal heresies, began with what its adherents believed to be a revival of the gift of prophecy. An even more tragic case would be Jim Jones's People's Temple disaster in the 1980s in which hundreds of people died by suicide. Another sad example strikes closer to home. The church building my congregation currently owns was purchased and remodeled in the early 1990s by a false prophet who moved his entire congregation from California to Denver, used their labor and money to refurbish the building and then sold it and absconded with the money.

Even within genuine Christian circles people can latch onto a gifted or charismatic man or woman and then stand on the words of that gifted one rather than on the eternal Word of God. I respect the ministry of Rick Joyner, for instance, and know him to be a genuine man of God and a dedicated student of Scripture. But many well-intentioned believers wait with tense anticipation for every issue of Rick's *MorningStar Journal* to arrive and then read it more faithfully and consistently than they do the Bible. This is certainly not Rick's fault or desire! But when believers place prophetic people in such elevated positions, only a secure and settled prophet can resist the temptation to begin to believe one's own press. For this reason, accountability for prophetic people runs high!

Too often the Church fails to test the prophetic word against Scripture. Delusions result, as the once pure anointing mutates into a counterfeit anointing divorced from the one foundation in Jesus. In various places over the years, as fascination with prophetic words has grown at the expense of the eternal Word of God, adulteries have resulted. People have actually believed God told them to divorce their mates and marry others. One man I know is currently imprisoned because of mistakes he made when overconfidence in his ability to hear accurately from God, combined with a failure to cling to Jesus and His eternal Word, led him astray.

As was the case with Jim Jones, some prophets seeking honor and control because of their insecurity and need for recognition can begin to abuse those under them. They regard prophetic ministry as a badge of stature bringing them personal power and significance. Particularly vulnerable are those whose early wounds of rejection have yet to be healed. What perhaps began with genuine gifting can end in delusions of grandeur.

A man who called himself a warning prophet, for example, joined a charismatic church, made a play for power and judged the people for their supposed failings. When they refused to fall down and worship at the idol of his exalted opinion of his own authority, he shook the dust off his feet and left, pronouncing judgments and destruction. He came as a man with a great deal of money. A year later he declared bankruptcy and ended up selling used cars for a living. Delusions of grandeur lead inevitably to destruction.

When my father's book *The Elijah Task* first came out in the 1970s, throngs of prophetic "wannabes" with delusions of prophetic exaltation wrote him reams and reams of prophetic garbage, hoping he would recognize, validate and exalt them. One actually showed up at my parents' home to inform them that she was coming to live with them and be their disciple. "God" had told her this. She was incensed and offended when they said, "Pardon us, but we don't think so!"

In short, bad prophetic words and deluded practitioners can cause a great deal of damage both to themselves and to the Church. I know of more than one congregation that identified itself as "prophetic" in its emphasis that no longer exists because of failure to guard against these dangers. Imbalance and delusion too often gain entry through a window of insecurity. Prophetic self-importance serves to cover up unresolved pain.

Taking the Lord's Name in Vain

Because being prophetic seems to be the latest "wannabe" obsession in the Body of Christ, "God told me" echoes from the walls of nearly every Spirit-filled church I know. People run to prophesy to one another, saying, "I have a word for you." Internet forums are filled with posts containing line after line of vapid emptiness written in first person, supposedly flowing from the mouth of God. The majority of this stuff is inaccurate, inconsistent and without real substance.

Deuteronomy 5:11 contains a sobering warning in connection with speaking presumptively in the Lord's name: "You shall not take the name of the LORD your God in vain, for the LORD will not leave him unpunished who takes His name in vain." Traditionally, we have understood this to mean that we must not use the Lord's name in connection with profanity. This is true. But *in vain* actually means "without purpose" or "void of anything useful or good." The point is that we must not speak a word in the name of the Lord, claiming that the word comes from Him, when it is not, in fact, His word. The temptation to carelessly invoke the Lord's name belies a fear of not being heard by others that leads us to try to bolster the force of our words at the Lord's expense. Words that claim to be His but are not are spoken "in vain"—to no purpose—and they invite His disciplining judgment.

It is much better to adopt a more humble stance and say, "I *think* the Lord may be saying," or "I have a sense that maybe the Lord is saying," rather than to invoke the Lord's name "in vain" and incur the judgment that comes from making a false claim. In too many places we are franchising irresponsibility and inviting punishment by encouraging those who are not prophetic to act and speak as though they were.

"But the prophet who speaks a word presumptuously in My name which I have not commanded him to speak, or which he speaks in the name of other gods, that prophet shall die" (Deuteronomy 18:20). In the New Testament Church we do not put people to death, but the sternness of the warning remains. It would be a wise move toward balance if we heard less of "God told me" in the charismatic wing of the Church and more of "I think maybe God is saying."

True Prophecy Is Undergirded with Humility

"Prophets" who have taken stands on personal revelation, as opposed to standing on the eternal written Word of the

Lord, can often be recognized by the negative ways they respond when challenged. When pride is threatened, false prophets take offense. Offense taken indicates lack of humility. Note the following examples.

I recall an incident in which one who thought herself prophetic demanded to speak a prophetic word to the congregation. Exercising his God-ordained protective role, her pastor demanded to know the content before granting approval. She insisted that God had told her not to reveal the content until she stood before the congregation. Of course, the pastor wisely denied her the microphone. She took offense and left the church in anger shortly after that.

I sometimes visit prophetic forums on the Internet. In one case a desperately hurting pastor posted a prayer request concerning a difficult financial situation precipitated in part by the departure of some troublemakers from his congregation and the turmoil they had stirred up before leaving. About half the "prophetic" respondents posted analyses of the problem under the guise of giving prophetic words. Some called on the pastor to repent for the sin they saw "prophetically" in his life and ministry, although they knew nothing of him and had never met him face to face. When confronted with the errors of fact inherent in their words and the ways in which they had completely missed the need of the moment, they took offense and further condemned the hapless pastor, who had asked only for prayer support. He stood accused of being blockheaded and arrogant for refusing the word of the Lord.

A man received a prophecy that he would be a great pastor. In response to this he sold his home, left his job and moved to another state to join a movement that seemed to promise the unfolding of this destiny. Given opportunity in the local church, he repeatedly failed to gather a stable group of any kind. People quietly but consistently refused to respond to his leadership. When the senior pastor denied him a position on the basis of that failure and refused him the platform in worship services, both he and his wife took offense, protesting loudly that the leadership of this church simply could not see how gifted he really was. The wiser and more humble thing would have been for him to recognize his limitations and realize that the prophetic word had some holes in it. Personal heartbreak and disharmony in the church resulted.

I wonder how much of this destruction should be regarded as the penalty prescribed in Deuteronomy 5:11 for taking the name of the Lord in vain? Certainly death in some form results—the prophet's "word" itself wreaks death and destruction, the prophet is cut off from the Body and relationships die. How much could be avoided if the prophet would adopt a more humble stance that would allow for challenging and testing?

Humility undergirds all good prophecy. Prophets must never allow themselves to take a stand on personal dreams, visions, words or perceptions as if these could not be challenged. The contemporary prophetic word can never be exempt from correction and testing.

The Need for Testing

Because it passes through the filter of the minds and hearts of those through whom it comes (see the earlier definition), every prophetic word takes on the color of the vessel through which it flows. This is why Jeremiah reads differently than Isaiah, and Micah contrasts with Zechariah in style. The personality of the prophet imprints upon the delivery of the word because God never bypasses the vessel through whom He speaks. Words come through the filter of our individual natures, which are both redeemed by Jesus and polluted by sin. Except for prophecies of Scripture, therefore, no word is ever so pure as to be exempt from testing. "Let two or three prophets speak, and let the others pass judgment" (1 Corinthians 14:29).

Here are seven tests for prophetic words.

Test #1: Does this supposed word from God stand the test of Scripture?

God has spoken once for all and with finality in the written Word. No valid prophetic word will ever convey new revelation not contained in the Scriptures, nor will it in any way contradict the written Word.

Colossians 2:18 warns the one who takes a "stand on visions he has seen, inflated without cause by his fleshly mind." We must never stand on personal revelation above what the Bible tells us. This verse also speaks of arrogance—a character flaw that, as we have already discussed, is common among people with prophetic leanings and wounds of rejection.

At the height of the prophetic movement in the 1980s, John Wimber gave this balancing word: "The only word God is obligated to fulfill is this Book." We may receive certain kinds of guidance through prophetic words delivered by reliably prophetic people, but we must not build our lives on those words. The Scriptures never disappoint, but the words of men often can, even when we believe they come from God. We must stake our lives on the eternal Word of God alone, while we thoroughly test everything else.

Test #2: Does this word reflect the revealed nature and character of God?

This again points us to the Bible, where the final revelation has been recorded for all the ages. We can begin this test with

1 John 4:8: "The one who does not love does not know God, for God is love." God *is* love. His love may take many forms, ranging from tenderness to discipline and even anger, but always it is love for our sake. We must study to understand the nature of that love so that we can instinctively discern whether or not a supposed prophetic word reflects the true nature and character of God.

Test #3: Does this word line up with what God is already doing and with what the Bible tells us God wants to do?

We must question words that lead us in different directions than those already in evidence in our lives and ministries. For instance, the church I pastor was founded on a vision for mercy—that we would be a place of refuge and healing. But many prophetic words from supposed prophetic people over the years moved us into a warfare focus. The result was predictably wounding. Until God brought about a cleansing, removed the competing voices and restored us to the original vision, warfare nearly destroyed us. We should have known.

If a major evangelistic thrust is bearing fruit in a city in accord with the Acts 1 commission to reach the nations, I would question any word that said to stop and begin to focus in another place. Besides, Scripture commands us to preach the Gospel and to make disciples. No subsequent word can be allowed to negate that command!

If pastors are coming together in unity and burying their differences in accord with the clear command of Scripture to be of one mind, I would seriously doubt the divine origin of a prophecy that told them to go their own ways. Scripture commands unity!

Test #4: Does it pass the reality check?

In my book *Purifying the Prophetic*, I told the story of a so-called prophetic woman who claimed she had a word that I was a great man of God but that I had the flaw of Jimmy Swaggart. In the 1980s, at the height of his international influence and evangelistic outreach, Jimmy Swaggart was caught twice with prostitutes. This woman meant that I had a weakness for temptation where women were concerned. If she had subjected her word to a reality check, she would have learned that in all my years of marriage since 1972 I have never been tempted. From the time I met Beth, no other woman has ever presented real allure for me. This woman's "prophetic word" would have run aground on the shoals of the reality check.

In another case a man who believed himself to be prophetic came to me with a word that a group of men would soon approach me seeking a financial alliance but that I should not ally with them because it would lead to financial ruin for the church. This "word" did not pass the reality check in two areas. First, my refusal over the years to treat wealthy people any differently than others has lost the church a lot of money, so the likelihood that I would make any kind of financial alliance involving the church is remote at best. The second is that no such group of men has ever approached me, despite the fact that several years have passed since that word was delivered.

What if someone were to come to me with a prophetic word that God was about to judge our church for its lack of care for the poor? I would have only to look to our Missions and Community Impact team to know the truth of it.

Reality checks could save us a great deal of heartache and confusion if only we would take the time to think and critically examine.

Test #5: Do any concrete realities accompany the prophetic word?

Finally, when receiving guidance or direction, I have come to value concrete realities embedded in the revelation itself that confirm the accuracy of what is being heard or prophesied. When God called Moses to go to Egypt and tell Pharaoh to let the people go, He gave him a burning bush—a real bush in real flames. When the apostle Paul received his call, he saw a bright light and heard an audible voice. Others saw the light and heard the voice, as well. These were real manifestations! They were concrete realities. Granted, these signs seem rare, but they do happen.

For instance, in May 2006 I performed the wedding of my oldest daughter's father-in-law. At the beginning of the wedding a thunderstorm gathered overhead. As I prayed the opening prayer, it grew in strength. As I administered the vows, God accentuated the groom's "I do" with a resounding thunderclap, then accommodated the bride's with a slightly smaller one, right on cue. As I began to deliver the prophetic word God had given me for them, lightning flashed and a deafening roar of thunder forced me to wait it out in order to be heard. Random thunder could have been ignored, but thunder on cue—not once but three times—could not be discounted. I will take a confirmation any way I can get it!

I believe the thunderclaps over that wedding ceremony were concrete realities God used to announce and confirm His approval for this couple's union. The moment I declared them man and wife and said "Amen," the storm stopped. The Lord has big things in store for that precious couple who found one another so late in life!

Test #6: Where prediction is part of the word, fulfillment becomes the determining test of validity.

It has often been said that a true word will confirm something we are already thinking, considering or feeling. Nowhere in Scripture can such a test be found. Too often the supposed prophet has only sensed what was already in the heart of the one to whom he was "prophesying" and has then reflected it back as a word from God without discerning the difference between what comes from the heart of God and what has its source in the heart of the human being.

The defining test in Scripture is therefore always fulfillment, even in cases where prediction is not the content. We must ask whether the supposed prophetic word released the power to accomplish something or whether it tore down something that needed tearing down. Did it have an impact that accomplished the purposes of God and connected the hearer with Jesus? Did it truly edify, or did it fail in that regard, either by taking up useless air space or by destroying something that should not have been destroyed?

> "You may say in your heart, 'How will we know the word which the LORD has not spoken?' When a prophet speaks in the name of the LORD, if the thing does not come about or come true, that is the thing which the LORD has not spoken. The prophet has spoken it presumptuously; you shall not be afraid of him."
>
> Deuteronomy 18:21–22

Test #7: Whom does it exalt?

"For the testimony of Jesus is the spirit of prophecy" (Revelation 19:10). Need I say more? True prophetic words strengthen us in our relationship with Jesus and in some way reveal who He is.

3

WHAT PROPHETIC MINISTRY IS NOT

I n addition to understanding what constitutes genuine prophetic ministry, every believer should also know what prophetic ministry is not. Such knowledge can serve to dispel much unnecessary confusion concerning this vital gift.

Prophetic Ministry Is Not a Bible Substitute

We have discussed how one of the tests for a prophetic word is whether or not it lines up with Scripture. We have learned that the Church must never allow herself to live for the prophetic word unless its content is written in Scripture. Even more important than this, contemporary prophetic ministry must never become a substitute for the Bible. Our sustenance and nourishment flow from the Holy Spirit and the authoritative and perfect revelation of the Bible.

In the same way that contemporary prophetic ministry cannot add to or substitute for Scripture, neither can it be made into a key for *interpreting* the Bible. The Bible must be interpreted and understood in its own context and on its own terms according to the intended meaning of the author. Four different contexts reveal this meaning.

First, every word of Scripture has a *linguistic context* that demands we study the original languages. Words have specific definitions that can be discovered.

Second, every verse has a *historical context*. Its meaning should be viewed in light of the events of the day, or historical backdrop, in which it was written.

Third, every passage of Scripture speaks from a *cultural context*. This context determines meaning in the same way that culture informs the meaning of words we use today.

And fourth, we must understand the passage in the *context of the verses surrounding it*. Context informs meaning. When we lift a verse from its context, we not only miss parts of its meaning, but we also often distort or even lose its true meaning entirely.

Careful study of each element of context therefore reveals the intended meaning of the author. That intended meaning is the only infallible revelation of God. We have no right to change it, spiritualize it or make it say anything other than it was originally intended to say. No level of supposed Holy Spirit inspiration can be allowed to supersede these considerations, or else we have granted ourselves the right to make the Bible say whatever we want it to say. Doing so takes God off the throne and presumptuously seats us in His place.

Scripture gives us an objective revelation that cannot be altered, not a subjective one that varies with the inner perception or personal inspiration of the reader. No revelation, prophetic word, dream or vision can change the intended meaning of any verse of Scripture. Personal revelation, prophetic words, dreams and visions can expand our understanding at the level of the heart, but they cannot be allowed to alter or even add to the message.

The problem is that for all the reasons outlined in chapter 1, we prophetic people tend to be intuitive. We reason with our feelings at the expense of rationality and logic. We think emotionally and must struggle to achieve a balance between the discipline of reason and the depth of wisdom that intuitive understanding can bring when such a balance exists. We need objective revelation, and Scripture provides this as we learn to study it properly.

Modern Prophets Do Not Have Authority to Command

New Testament prophets do not carry the same level of authority as the Old Testament prophets did. Samuel, for example, delivered instructions from heaven and rightly expected King Saul to obey them. Old Testament prophets represent God's own authority.

By contrast, New Testament prophets serve *under* the Church's established leaders and authority structures. In the book of Acts Agabus informed Paul that if he went to Jerusalem he would be arrested (see Acts 21:10–11). He stopped short of commanding Paul. Rather, Agabus simply transmitted prophetic information, rightly leaving it up to Paul to decide what to do. Having been informed by the prophetic word, Paul chose to go to Jerusalem and be arrested anyway. But he went prepared by the word Agabus had given him, knowing what would happen and how he would use those events and circumstances to advance the Gospel. He then appealed to the emperor and preached the Gospel to every government official he encountered along the way.

A budding and immature prophetic person had a dream in which the elders of his church were building a great building. Not understanding the limitations of his authority, he interpreted his dream to mean that the church must start a building project. Subsequently he moved through the congregation declaring this call to a building project as a word from the Lord. By the time this got back to the pastor and the church board, his words had generated a controversy. The pastor and the board knew that the current facility was inadequate, but they also knew what the young prophet did not know—that the fellowship lacked the cohesion necessary to take on a building project. The church *body* needed to be built up and strengthened, covenant needed to be established, leaders had to be trained and deployed and so on. That was the meaning of the symbolism in the young prophet's dream.

It is not the role of New Testament prophetic people to command or set direction. Their task is to submit their revelations to the appointed authorities and then allow those authorities to decide what to do with them.

Prophetic Ministry Is Not to Be Equated with Mystical Experiences

Among the biblical prophets, mystical experiences are only one means of receiving divine revelation. Such experiences actually comprise a relatively small portion of the prophetic books of the Bible and are mostly confined to apocalyptic passages in portions of Daniel, parts of Ezekiel, parts of Zechariah and the book of Revelation. Ezekiel is not considered a greater prophet than Jeremiah for the frequency of wild visions he received, nor is the apostle John (author of the book of Revelation) exalted above the apostle Paul for the same reason.

Scripture shows prophetic people seeking the mind and heart of God, but not necessarily with a specific experience in mind. Nothing in the text of Revelation, for instance, indicates that the apostle John actively sought to be caught up in dramatic visions. Scripture says only that he was "in the Spirit on the Lord's day" (Revelation 1:10) and that God sovereignly chose to visit him with powerful heavenly visions.

Unfortunately in the Church today there is a trend toward seeking ways and means to generate these experiences by our own initiative. We tend to exalt those who have these experiences as if they were more holy, more spiritual, more gifted or more prophetically reliable than others. This is a dangerous imbalance and an improper focus. Better to hunger after simple and pure intimacy with the Holy Spirit than to focus on any given result of that intimacy or means of receiving revelation. In Scripture, prayer, meditation and worship seem to be the key means of finding that intimacy.

Isaiah experienced the great Temple vision of Isaiah 6, but such visions were neither the dominant feature of his prophetic revelation nor his primary means of receiving the Word. God did not promise mystical experiences to Jeremiah when He called him as a prophet. He simply declared in Jeremiah 1:9, "Behold, I have put My words in your mouth." I strongly suspect that He did this through the Holy Spirit by means of character adjustments and through the study of Scripture, as Jeremiah took into himself the substance and sense of all God had revealed of Himself up until that time. Because of this it became possible for him to hear the voice of the Lord in an intimate, practical and natural way, which is reflected in the record of his words.

Some prophets are spinning out of balance. We do this for two reasons. One is that our intuitive natures predispose us to be open to supernatural experiences. By itself this does not necessarily present a problem. The problem comes with the second reason. By becoming caught up in and fascinated by supernatural experiences, we can anesthetize the pain so many of us carry. Consequently, prophets can tend to subconsciously hunger for the experiences themselves, rather than for genuine and simple intimacy with God.

By aspiring after the mystical realms in an unbalanced way, we open ourselves to delusion and demonic counterfeit. Seeking by any human method to have a revelatory dream, for instance, is out of order and borders on occult practice.

It is much better to aspire after intimacy with the One who gives us dreams as He chooses to give us dreams. In fact, Ecclesiastes 5:7 teaches, "For in many dreams and in many words there is emptiness. Rather, fear God." Mystical experiences cannot be equated with fellowship with God. It would therefore be wrong to actively seek to have visions or to employ any method or approach to produce them. Better to long to be included in the intimate counsel of the Lord who sometimes sovereignly chooses a vision as one means of conveying His counsel.

In Acts 8:40 God teleported Philip over some considerable distance, but this was a sovereign act of God and not something Philip went looking for by any prayer or method. Philip had been with the Ethiopian eunuch on the road to Gaza. God needed him instantly at Azotus, and so He sovereignly moved him there by His own means and for His own purposes.

Over and over today I hear and see prophetic people writing and speaking openly of their "third heaven" experiences. The apostle Paul wrote:

I know a man in Christ who fourteen years ago—whether in the body I do not know, or out of the body I do not know, God knows—such a man was caught up to the third heaven. And I know how such a man—whether in the body or apart from the body I do not know, God knows—was caught up into Paradise and heard inexpressible words, which a man is not permitted to speak.

2 Corinthians 12:2–4

On the basis of what Paul wrote, I question how many of these "third heaven" experiences we hear about today are biblically legal to reveal to others. In addition, such sharing creates an unhealthy fascination with experiences that are not normally available to the average believer and diverts attention from weightier and more important aspects of the Christian walk, such as the mystery of the cross, the wonder of God's love and pure servanthood in intimacy with God. Sharing such experiences openly also serves to make the prophet appear unduly powerful and important in the eyes of others and can therefore become yet another cover for deep insecurities and the need to be seen as important.

To be clear, I personally love mystical experiences. I have been literally paralyzed by the presence of God for an hour and a half, my face and extremities turned numb by His power penetrating and healing me. I lay helpless on the floor and wept until the tears ran dry. Angels have visited me three times, twice to deliver instructional guidance from heaven and once for healing after a surgery. I love these experiences, but I have determined never to seek any such encounter of my own volition or by any learned method originating with me. That would be occult practice and magic. The initiative for that kind of thing lies with my God.

Actually, many who seem to have such experiences on a regular basis are not prophetic or holy at all but have simply opened themselves up spiritually by some human approach or through natural abilities to sense things in the realm of the spirit (note the small *s*). One need not, therefore, be holy or pure to have a supernatural experience. Witches and warlocks have supernatural experiences. New Agers have supernatural experiences. Shamans and witch doctors have supernatural experiences. Each of them understands and practices some kind of method to produce these things.

When Philip encountered Simon in Samaria, Scripture says Simon was one who

> formerly was practicing magic in the city and astonishing the people of Samaria, claiming to be someone great; and they all, from smallest to greatest, were giving attention to him, saying, "This man is what is called the Great Power of God." And they were giving him attention because he had for a long time astonished them with his magic arts.
>
> Acts 8:9–11

Simon was adept at producing psychic and supernatural experiences, but as Peter so aptly put it in Acts 8:21, "You have no part or portion in this matter, for your heart is not right before God."

God can and does use mystical experiences to convey revelation. But openness to experience mystical things in the spirit realm does not equate with prophetic calling or ability, although many genuinely prophetic people do have such experiences, some of them frequently. If the initiative lies with God and not with you, take all you can get! My plea is for character formation at the cross in union with Jesus and a pure hunger after intimacy with God into which He can pour whatever forms of experience He sovereignly chooses. We prophetic people tend to engage in enthusiastic imbalance, and I would remedy that.

Prophetic Ministry Is Not "Sanctified Psychic Reading"

Since we are created in His image, every one of us has a personal spirit given by God. One of the essential functions of the personal spirit is to enable us to identify with others at the level of spirit.

The word *compassion* has two parts. *Com* means "with." *Passion* means "to feel." Compassion, "to feel with," is the birthright of every human being. We feel with one another through a divinely created interconnection.

On the basis of this essential attribute of humanity indwelt by the Holy Spirit in the life of the believer, Paul said, "For by one Spirit we were all baptized into one body, whether Jews or Greeks, whether slaves or free, and we were all made to drink of one Spirit" (1 Corinthians 12:13). Then in verse 26 he added, "And if one member suffers, all the members suffer with it; if one member is honored, all the members rejoice with it." In Galatians 6:2 he commanded us to "bear one another's burdens, and thereby fulfill the law of Christ."

Which of us has not at some time entered a room full of people and instantly sensed the mood of those in it before a word was ever spoken? Which of us has not sat down with a friend and known instinctively that something was wrong despite the smiles and the jokes? To accurately perceive what is in the heart of another person does not make us prophetic. It makes us human. The more alive we become in our spirits, the more alert and sensitive we become to the hearts of those around us. This is our birthright as persons created in God's image until and unless cultural influences or spiritual and emotional wounds cripple us.

Some of us seem to be prodigies at sensing the hearts of others, in the same way that some of us run faster than others, have a better sense for music or an aptitude for mathematics. We often exalt people who possess this innate sense to the status of "prophet," thinking that they could know what they know from the hearts and lives of others only if God told them. Not so. We need only be fully alive in our spirits. Any of us can sense these things, and any of us can learn to sense such things better as we come alive in our spirits. Virtually all prophetic people are prodigies at this kind of sensitivity, but not all who are prodigies at this kind of sensitivity are prophetic.

Trouble comes when we believe we are being prophetic and we sense ambition, desire or hope in the heart of another, assume that it must be something God is saying and then present it as a "prophecy" when all we are really doing is mirroring what is already in that heart. Prophecy is words from God to men and women, not a reading of the hearts and minds of men and women by men and women. Prophecy must be the fruit of intimacy with God on the part of the one who prophesies, not the result of personal psychic awareness.

Our human ability to feel with others, to identify with them at the level of spirit, is the foundation of real compassion and can be a wonderful tool for ministry, but we must not confuse it with being prophetic. Wonderful prophetic words, on the other hand, can result as we compassionately identify with the hearts of others, accurately read what is there from the human side and then turn to seek God for the true word in relation to it. Knowing the difference between the desire we sense in the heart of the one to whom we are ministering and the word flowing from the heart of God differentiates between the true and the false prophetic word in one-on-one prophetic ministry. Maturity, experience, brokenness and humility acquired over time enable us to differentiate what we sense in the hearts of people from the true word flowing from the heart of God. Unfortunately, few of us have even been made aware of the difference, much less the need to seek this level of discernment.

In 1 Kings 22 four hundred prophets sensed the desire of the kings, Ahab and Jehoshaphat, to go to war and reflected it back to them as a prophetic word from God assuring victory. Apparently only Micaiah had the capacity through intimacy with the Lord to discern the difference between the desire in the heart of the kings and the true heart of God. He warned them not to go, and they threw him in jail for his unwillingness to tell them what they wanted to hear. In the ensuing battle Ahab was killed—all because of failure to understand the difference between a sanctified psychic reading of the hearts of men and the true word of the Lord flowing from His intimate counsel. Worse, that failure enabled a lying spirit (see 1 Kings 22:22) to enter the prophets and deceive all four hundred of them.

Failure to discern this difference between psychic reading and the word flowing from the heart of God sets us up to hear from the enemy of our souls and ultimately leads to destruction. Sanctified psychic reading can be a wonderful tool in compassionate ministry under the discipline of the Holy Spirit, but we must never confuse it with being truly prophetic.

Prophetic Ministry Is Not Warfare

Many supposed prophetic people seem always to be looking for a fight, as if to be prophetic could be equated with being engaged in spiritual warfare. Why would we assume that prophetic people must be warriors? I have known and loved a number of prophetic people who erroneously made that assumption concerning themselves. In every case it has led to forms of destruction, self-importance and abuse of others.

On occasion prophetic people may be forced to go to war when circumstances make warfare necessary. Elijah, for example, faced down and slew the 450 prophets of Baal (see 1 Kings 18). On an infinitely lesser scale, I have been there and done that! But warfare must never be the focus of the prophetic life.

Over the years some have attempted to impose on me a warrior identity. At one point they had me convinced, but the result was death and delusion—alienation from God and from my true calling—and I will not walk that way again. If the heart of the prophet is for intimacy with God and if Jesus is the Prince of Peace, then what does that teach us about our nature and purpose as prophetic people? Look deep into the writings of the biblical prophets and you will find tender hearts, broken for God and broken for Israel. They were lovers first and warriors only when they had to be.

We have now examined what prophetic ministry is and is not. Let's take a still deeper look at the prophetic task.

4

THE PROPHETIC TASK

The clearest single New Testament definition of the prophetic task is Paul's instruction in 1 Corinthians 14:3: "But one who prophesies speaks to men for edification and exhortation and consolation." We have already looked at this verse as a definition of prophetic ministry. Now let's focus on the individual descriptive words Paul uses and consider the specific tasks of the prophet in the Church.

Edification

Edification refers to the act of building up. A true prophetic word therefore serves to build, enlarge or strengthen those for whom it is intended and has a positive effect on the ministry of the Church, its fellowship and its cohesiveness. It may be a clearly affirming word, or it may be corrective or confrontational, but even in correction and confrontation the result must be strengthening.

71

It was 1990. The time had come to leave both the church I had planted and the ministry I had pursued with my family for twelve years, Elijah House, in Post Falls, Idaho. I did not want to go. More accurately, I was filled with fear of *letting go*, even as the Lord sovereignly shrank both the church and my role at Elijah House. I grew more disheartened and miserable by the day. Finally my associate pastor, who had an occasional prophetic gift, came to my office, took a seat before me and issued the challenge: "Loren, what are you still doing here?" He then catalogued for me the waste of my gifts that staying in Post Falls represented and castigated me for being afraid to move. His loving confrontation of my destructive obsession with remaining where I no longer belonged built me up and strengthened me for the changes that had to come. This was edification.

In another instance, in 1989 Bob Jones called me aside at a pastors' conference to speak first into my calling, affirming offices yet to be held, and then into gifts both currently practiced and yet to be developed. Next he told me, "Time for you to feel, boy! Time to let feelings live." I had been emotionally locked up, unable to grieve a number of losses I had suffered over a long period of time. This had imprisoned most of my other feelings, as well, so that I had become emotionally unavailable both to my family and to those to whom I ministered professionally. Bob's words planted hope, clarified direction and strengthened me to move forward both emotionally and in ministry: edification.

I experienced some difficult days of wounding and grieving after that, but Bob's words set in motion a release of healing that helped to sustain me over the next fifteen years. Through some difficult years of change, I was able to hold onto the words he had spoken concerning my calling and destiny and from them draw some of the strength I needed to endure and process the pain I carried. His words edified me, built me up and helped carry me through.

When Paul wrote of edification, he often placed the emphasis on the church as a fellowship. Prophetic people must therefore cultivate an awareness of the need to leave a prophetic deposit that edifies the Church by deepening interpersonal connections and bonding the hearts of the people with their pastors, as well as the hearts of the pastors with the people. Such a word can be openly positive, but it also can be confrontational or corrective.

Joe King, for example, a prophetic teacher and worship leader from Great Britain, visits our church every year. In late 2005 I turned over our Sunday evening renewal service to him for worship, teaching and ministry. He rightly discerned that an old spirit of criticism that had significantly damaged us over the years had been dramatically reduced, but that a small and limited undercurrent remained. After speaking of this openly, he called us into a time of ministry in which he provided an opportunity for people to come forward in repentance for having participated in that spirit and to renounce it once and for all. Specifically he called for people to come to my wife and me to confess any participation in the critical spirit and to commit to stand with us. A powerful time of bonding and rebonding resulted and we were edified, strengthened and built up as a people. True prophetic ministry has this kind of effect, even when confrontation of sin is involved.

Ernie Freeman works with Streams Ministries under John Paul Jackson. While teaching their course "201—Understanding Dreams and Visions" at our church in 2004, he suddenly stopped and began to prophesy openly concerning our fellowship. As he spoke, my fingers flew over the keys on my laptop computer to record his words as he spoke them. The following is my transcription:

A farm field. A farm field and not a fallow field. Deep and consistent plowing where the ground has been prepared. A huge vast field where the ground has been prepared and tilled. Dark and rich soil. And it is now the exact moment for the planting of the seed. The whole field is quivering for the planting. This is the jack-in-the-beanstalk church with the magical seeds that spring up overnight—large, huge and rising straight up into the heavenly realm. People will be able to climb right into the heavenly presence on the beanstalk.

A year and a half passed before the fulfillment began to manifest, but as I write, the very things Ernie spoke have begun to unfold. God spoke to him to edify us, to strengthen us in hope and to release a measure of power to bring our congregational destiny to pass. True prophetic words leave this kind of deposit.

Exhortation

Exhortation is a word for stirring things up and for calling individuals and churches to a specific and concrete action. In Peter's sermon in Acts 2, for instance, he "kept on exhorting them, saying, 'Be saved from this perverse generation!'" (Acts 2:40). Peter specifically invited them to repent and be baptized, promising the gift of the Holy Spirit as a result.

Paul did a similar thing in 1 Thessalonians 2:11–12, when he stirred up the believers in Thessalonica and called them to action—to "walk in a manner worthy":

Just as you know how we were exhorting and encouraging and imploring each one of you as a father would his own children, so that you would walk in a manner worthy of the God who calls you into His own kingdom and glory.

First Corinthians 1:10 contains another example of exhortation to action: "Now I exhort you, brethren, by the name of our Lord Jesus Christ, that you all agree and that there be no divisions among you, but that you be made complete in the same mind and in the same judgment." Again, Paul exhorted them and stirred them to a specific action.

In 1974, as a student at Fuller Theological Seminary, I took a part-time position as youth director in a church not far from the original Calvary Chapel, which is widely recognized as the birthplace of contemporary Christian music. As often as I could, I took my youth group to Saturday night concerts there. After every concert there was an evangelistic sermon and an altar call for those who wanted to give their lives to Jesus. Most of the crowd would then go home while a remnant remained for the "afterglow," a time of simple worship accompanied by words of knowledge and healing. Although I had grown up in the charismatic renewal, I had not received the gift of tongues—until one night as the Spirit fell in an afterglow at Calvary Chapel. The glory descended on me during worship, and I began to sing in a language I had never heard. I should have continued to use the gift in my daily devotions, but it felt strange to me. I worried that it was not real, and so I stopped.

Not long after that, two people who were unrelated to one another and unaware of my struggle brought me prophetic words with exactly the same content and within the same week. Paraphrased, the message went something like this: "You have received the gift of tongues, but you have not been using it. You *must* use it, whether it feels strange to you or not, because you need the strengthening it brings." This was prophetic exhortation and encouragement intended to inspire me to take specific action. I have been praying in tongues on a daily basis ever since—and it has long since ceased to feel strange.

Consolation

In the original Greek the word *consolation* refers to the kind of comfort that helps alleviate grief. Consolation settles the shattered and tumultuous emotions that accompany wounding or loss. In the context of edification and exhortation, however, this seems too narrow an application for Paul's purposes. The application, if not the meaning, must therefore be expanded.

Usually significant change, great advances or great callings are preceded not by seasons of ease and obvious favor but by times of turmoil. Scripture often calls these times "birth pangs" or "travail," likening the pain to the difficulty of giving birth (see Isaiah 66:8; Matthew 24:8; Mark 13:8; Romans 8:22). Suffering causes confusion, especially when it follows on the heels of prophetic words of promise. In this light, edification and exhortation can be followed by seasons of travail, confusion and grief before new things are birthed!

My own church endured a significant season of travail in the year following Ernie Freeman's word to us. Sin and deception came to light, and I was forced to take strong corrective action. People left us. We fell behind financially. All this constituted a necessary form of birth pain preceding the time of release and growth. Much of it left us struggling with hurt and confusion.

Paul wrote about the consolation that settles and makes sense of the grief caused by the turmoil and pain preceding the realization of divine calling or breakthrough. The prophet clarifies what is happening and settles the hearts of the people so that grief and hurt cannot derail the wonderful purposes of God. The new thing must be born. Part of a prophet's function is to focus the attention of the flock on the purpose beyond the turmoil.

Even the most cursory reading of such books as Isaiah, Jeremiah and Ezekiel reveals this function of comfort. Each one prophesied that suffering would come in the form of judgment for the sin of Israel, but at the same time each one proclaimed the promise of God to emerge afterward. The pain of cleansing would produce a glorious effect for the people of Israel.

Just one of many examples is Isaiah 54:1–8:

"Shout for joy, O barren one, you who have borne no child; break forth into joyful shouting and cry aloud, you who have not travailed; for the sons of the desolate one will be more numerous than the sons of the married woman," says the LORD. "Enlarge the place of your tent; stretch out the curtains of your dwellings, spare not; lengthen your cords and strengthen your pegs. For you will spread abroad to the right and to the left. And your descendants will possess nations and will resettle the desolate cities. Fear not, for you will not be put to shame; and do not feel humiliated, for you will not be disgraced; but you will forget the shame of your youth, and the reproach of your widowhood you will remember no more. For your husband is your Maker, whose name is the LORD of hosts; and your Redeemer is the Holy One of Israel, who is called the God of all the earth. For the LORD has called you, like a wife forsaken and grieved in spirit, even like a wife of one's youth when she is rejected," says your God. "For a brief moment I forsook you, but with great compassion I will gather you. In an outburst of anger I hid My face from you for a moment, but with everlasting lovingkindness I will have compassion on you," says the LORD your Redeemer.

A well-known older prophet once said to me, "You got a high calling, son. You got a lot more suffering to do." He made sense of the hurt I was experiencing in a preparatory time of pain.

The prophet makes sense of turmoil or suffering, gives it purpose and therefore settles the hearts of God's people. This is consolation.

Admonition

To admonish is to call to account for sin, either individual or corporate. It requires relationship in order to work properly. We all know how much easier it is to receive correction from one whose love you have experienced than it is to receive it from someone who has not paid the price to really know you.

The prophet Nathan, for example, confronted David with his adultery with Bathsheba and the murder of her husband, Uriah (see 2 Samuel 12), and David readily received it. The record shows that Nathan and David had enjoyed a respectful working relationship prior to this.

Isaiah 58 stands as a wonderful model for admonition. Although Isaiah confronted the sin of the nation, this chapter could not be characterized as negative in its tone. Isaiah spoke of Israel's confusion over why answers to their prayers were not forthcoming and explained that the cause was their sin. They had practiced contention and strife. They had tolerated all manner of sin and had become oppressors to their servants. The poor had been neglected. All this had formed a barrier between them and God so that their prayers were hindered. Yet preceding this in verse 2, Isaiah acknowledged Israel's desire for God: "Yet they seek Me day by day and delight to know My ways, as a nation that has done righteousness and has not forsaken the ordinance of their God. They ask Me for just decisions, they delight in the nearness of God." And following the confrontation of their sin, Isaiah gives them instruction: If Israel would feed the hungry, clothe the naked, honor the Sabbath and set free those they had oppressed, "then your light will break out like the dawn, and your recovery will speedily spring forth; and your righteousness will go before you; the glory of the LORD will be your rear guard" (verse 8). In the remaining verses the promise grows to include the rebuilding of the nation.

True admonition never stops with confrontation over sin, nor does it descend to mere statements of condemnation. Because the true prophetic word reflects the heart of God, who is love, it includes a way out and a promise of redemption and blessing.

Admonition confronts sin, calls for change and kindles hope. If it is true that "the testimony of Jesus is the spirit of prophecy" (Revelation 19:10), then the prophetic word must reflect not only the cross where our sin was judged, but also the resurrection where Jesus claimed the victory for our redemption. Admonition without the hope of redemption can only play into the hands of the accuser of our souls.

The Watchman

"Surely the Lord GOD does nothing unless He reveals His secret counsel to His servants the prophets" (Amos 3:7). Prophetic people serve as watchmen on the walls, seeing at a distance what the Lord is about to do and proclaiming it in order to prepare the people. Once again the example of Agabus in Acts 11:28 illustrates the point. He saw at a distance that famine was coming and warned the Church.

The Lord gave me a prophetic dream concerning our present congregation in which a long column of bedraggled people were flowing into our church building from the north like refugees from a war zone. I looked out over our sanctuary in the dream and lamented, "Lord, we're too few." He answered, "That's irrelevant. They're coming." For eight years I prayed about that dream until He again began to indicate through dream and vision, "Get ready; they're coming!" Obediently I began to preach and teach in ways that would prepare my people to open up to increase. I called our prayer people to pray concerning it. We strengthened our counseling department. Our Missions and Community Impact pastor set things in motion to beef up our food bank and clothes closet. We began to expand our cell group network. We got ready. And they came. Because the watchman "saw" it in advance, when the refugees began to come, we were more prepared than we had appeared to be in my dream.

The warning can be negative, as well, as the watchman assumes a protective role. He or she sees the enemy approaching and sounds the alarm.

More than once I have warned fellow pastors of the true nature of people transferring into their churches. Prophetically, I saw the trouble that would come if these people were allowed into sensitive areas of ministry. In some cases the warning was heeded. In others it was not, and destruction resulted. I am grateful for people in my own congregation who reliably alert me to the approach of individuals in whom danger lies. And there is a positive side to this function, too, as the prophet alerts the leadership of the church to the approach of people with right hearts who can use their gifts to edify. Paul called this gift "distinguishing of spirits" ("discerning of spirits" in some translations; see 1 Corinthians 12:10).

Another aspect of the warning function involves insight into the future. A watchman/prophet sees the sin of God's people, warns of the fruit it will bring and calls for repentance. For many years Jeremiah warned Israel concerning the judgment to come if the nation refused to turn, but he also included the promise:

> Hear the word of the LORD, O nations, and declare in the coastlands afar off, and say, "He who scattered Israel will gather him and keep him as a shepherd keeps his flock." For the LORD has ransomed Jacob and redeemed him from the hand of him who was stronger than he. "They will come and shout for joy on the height of Zion, and they will be radiant over the bounty of the LORD—over the grain and the new wine and the oil, and over the young of the flock and the herd; and their life will be like a watered garden, and they will never languish again. Then the virgin will rejoice in the dance, and the young men and the old, together, for I will turn their mourning into joy and will comfort them and give them joy for their sorrow. I will fill the soul of the priests with abundance, and My people will be satisfied with My goodness," declares the LORD.
>
> Jeremiah 31:10–14

So certain was Jeremiah of the promise he saw coming after the judgment that he spoke of it in the "prophetic present," declaring what was to come as if it were already a reality. Those able to hear him could therefore pass through the fires of judgment strengthened with a hope and a promise because of the Lord's preparatory words spoken through Jeremiah in his role as a watchman.

Our church had only recently navigated successfully an extended time of severe trial. Because such times can condition people to function in a less than positive mode, we found ourselves having difficulty transitioning to a time of peace from a time of spiritual warfare. Negatives clung stubbornly to us like lint on a good suit. In an evening intercessory meeting one of our prophetic people who served in the role of a watchman suddenly looked up with the light of revelation shining in her eyes and exclaimed, "I always thought that being a watchman meant warning about dangerous people coming over the horizon. I just realized that I've been stuck in looking for the negative and that it has blinded me to the positive. Worse, it has caused me to magnify shortcomings in people so that I couldn't see the good and love them. I've been one of the reasons we've had difficulty becoming a loving people." Watchmen see the positive workings of God coming, as well as those things that require warning, but how easy it is to be drawn to the negative!

One of the most common traps into which immature prophetic people can fall is this trap of wallowing in the negative. They may see sin more than they perceive progress against it. They may sense difficulty coming but cannot see through it to the promise on the other side. They may see demons on or in others more than the glow of the Holy Spirit. The tendency to stumble in this way may stem from their burden-bearing natures as the weight of what they sense from others overwhelms them. Sometimes it develops from a need to feel important, righteous, powerful and "in the know." Seeing others as weak, ignorant and sinful can be strong medication for a weak and rejected self-perception. Those in mentoring roles need to help these beginners sort out these things and point them toward the victory and grace we have in Jesus.

In summary, as watchmen we are called to see the hand of God at work, the unfolding of His plans approaching. We are *not* called to crush God's people with words of condemnation and judgment without hope.

Prophetic Portfolio

Speaking from experience and observation, prophetic people have different portfolios. We are often called and limited to specific times, places or spheres of influence. Samuel seemed to have sweeping authority over all Israel. His portfolio covered the whole nation in a governmental way. Nathan's portfolio seems to have been focused on bringing the Lord's word to King David: "In accordance with all these words and all this vision, so Nathan spoke to David" (2 Samuel 7:17); "Then the LORD sent Nathan to David" (2 Samuel 12:1). Accordingly, some prophetic people carry an anointing to speak the word of the Lord specifically for governmental authorities. The portfolio carried by Agabus in the New Testament seems to have been specifically to see into the future. Both of his recorded prophecies predicted things that would affect the Church deeply, and so he prepared the Body of Christ for things to come.

Some prophetic people are better at prophesying concerning events in nature than at dealing with people. Others function accurately and powerfully when dealing with governmental officials and issues, but less well when it comes to the Body of Christ or the world of nature. Some work powerfully when ministering prophetically to individuals but seem to miss it when it comes to the wider Body of Christ, government or nature.

Whether a prophetic person's portfolio is broad or narrow, general or specific, wisdom dictates that one understand the scope and limitation of his or her calling and humbly serve there. Many of us have gotten into trouble by assuming more portfolio than we have been given. Callings can evolve from little to much or from much back to little. In the end, we must maintain our intimacy with God and submit to whatever He calls us to do.

No matter what elements a prophetic person's portfolio holds, intercessory prayer will be part of it. While the following chapter makes no attempt at a comprehensive treatment of the subject of intercession, it does address some common pitfalls and imbalances.

5

THE PROPHET AS INTERCESSOR

Prophetic people tend to gravitate toward intercessory ministry because the calling inevitably draws them there. This is as it should be. If most prophetic people must remain hidden, then what they hear from God falls into the category of guidance for prayer. The chief role of prophetic people in intercessory groups is to receive revelation concerning direction for prayer. In fact, one key calling for prophetic people is to cry out to God on behalf of others on the basis of prophetic revelation and guidance. Although this revelation and guidance comes from heaven, earthbound pastoral guidance remains essential.

Pastoral Involvement

Given the inherent imbalance of most prophetic people when left to themselves, most pastors avoid the intercessory ministries of their churches, allowing them to function but holding them at a safe and comfortable distance. This is an unfortunate error. Intercessory ministries must serve the vision of the pastor, but with insufficient guidance, intercessory and prophetic people can quickly become the proverbial tail trying to wag the dog. If a pastor wishes the intercessory ministry of the church to edify the vision of the church, and if he wishes to gain prophetic insight from it, he or she must be directly involved in it, establishing pastoral presence and authority.

I am always in attendance and always in charge at the prayer meetings of our church. If I cannot be there, I make certain a trusted associate from our staff or lay leadership leads the meeting. One night I was out of town and the group met without me. On the walls at the back of the sanctuary were hung some banners that had been given to us by another congregation. These banners had been made at a time when that church was experiencing a time of division and pain. Our prophetic people felt this that night, but in the absence of the balance I would have brought to the meeting, they built up what they sensed into a frenzy of delusion and misplaced prophetic enthusiasm. Before long they had decided these banners were somehow demon-inhabited, so they took them outside the building and burned them. What began as a concern that could have been covered in prayer ended in wanton destruction of church property without permission from higher authority. And that does not even begin to address the questionable theological assumption that spirits can inhabit physical objects.

Intercessory prayer forms an essential part of what drives, energizes and informs the ministries of a church. But in order for it to remain on center, pastoral involvement is essential.

Getting the Words Right

Prophetic people tend to be word-oriented due to their need to clearly communicate to others what they have seen and heard. But the intuitive nature of these people often operates emotionally at the expense of the critical intellect. None of the prophetic people I know would say it this way, but the subtle assumption that creeps in is that if we must get our words right in order for *people* to understand us, then we must get our words right in order for *God* to hear us. As a result, prayer begins as an exercise in receiving revelation concerning what to pray about but can degenerate quickly into seeking revelation concerning how to pray—as if the words themselves create the reality or make God move.

When answers to prayer and the release of power depend upon the accuracy of our words, then we have left the realm of prayer and entered into magic. What began as relationship has degenerated into something mechanical—a casting of spells—as if we could push the right buttons and move God to act. God acts because He loves us, not because we got our words right. Heaven forbid that the power of God should be held hostage to our frail ability to understand!

It is, however, important to discern the will of God to the best of our ability and to align ourselves with it. "This is the confidence which we have before Him, that, if we ask anything according to His will, He hears us" (1 John 5:14). The purpose of prophetic ministry in intercession is neither to enforce nor to change the will of God but to reveal it for those praying who need to be aligned with Him.

Particularly in the Old Testament the heart of the prophetic task is to call the people out of idolatry and back to the Lord—to align them again with His will in obedience so as to stand them once more in the place of blessing. Second Chronicles 7:13–14 is often quoted as a mandate for intercessory prayer:

> "If I shut up the heavens so that there is no rain, or if I command the locust to devour the land, or if I send pestilence among My people, and My people who are called by My name humble themselves and pray and seek My face and turn from their wicked ways, then I will hear from heaven, will forgive their sin and will heal their land."

In the call to hear and reveal the will of God for prayer, a part of the prophetic task in intercession is to reveal the places where sin hides and to lead in repentance.

The Limits of Authority

Immature prophetic people, filled with the sense and power of the Lord's word—and sometimes full of themselves—often tend to overestimate the boundaries of their authority in prayer and credit themselves with more authority than they have been given. I have seen prophetic people calling things down from heaven with loud authoritative voices and summoning demonic powers before heavenly courts for judgment. This is foolish posturing. We have authority to call nothing down from heaven, to convene no heavenly court. Nowhere does Scripture set a precedent for these things, except perhaps in Elijah's encounter with the 450 prophets of Baal. Yet note the nature of Elijah's prayer:

> At the time of the offering of the evening sacrifice, Elijah the prophet came near and said, "O LORD, the God of Abraham, Isaac and Israel, today let it be known that You are God in Israel and that I am Your servant and I have done all these

things at Your word. Answer me, O LORD, answer me, that this people may know that You, O LORD, are God, and that You have turned their heart back again."

1 Kings 18:36–37

Immature prophetic people would have *commanded* fire to come from heaven, but Elijah did not pray that way. His prayer was the humble request of one who understood himself to be a servant exercising his position of relationship with the God who loved him. Not one word of command! He humbly asked God to glorify His own name by sending fire, and God responded.

Prophetic people speak the word of God to align God's people with His will and to bring humility and repentance. When praying seems blocked and the connection broken, the prophetic role is to discern why—to seek revelation regarding ways in which our ways differ from His. "If you abide in Me, and My words abide in you, ask whatever you wish, and it will be done for you" (John 15:7). The prophet exposes those ways in which we are not abiding.

A Special Class of People

A brief comment about the term *intercessors* seems in order. Nowhere does the Bible speak of or commission a special class of people called "intercessors," and yet today there seems to be a growing movement dedicated to doing just that. This may not seem dangerous until we examine the fruit. How we love to feel as if we have more power or authority before the throne than others! True? Those who are immature in their prophetic gifting tend to believe that they have more authority to be heard before the throne than those who are not so gifted. Their attitude becomes,

89

God hears intercessors better than He hears others. Give it to the intercessors, and they will get it done in prayer faster than others.

There are three problems with this new designation in the Body of Christ. First, nowhere in Scripture is anyone called an intercessor except Jesus and His Spirit. To intercede is to function as a go-between for two parties who need to connect. Jesus did that once and for all for us on the cross. He is our Intercessor. "Therefore He is able also to save forever those who draw near to God through Him, since He always lives to make intercession for them" (Hebrews 7:25).

Second, nowhere in Scripture do we find any leader in the Body of Christ calling on an elite body of intercessors to pray. When support is needed, they call upon the *Church* to pray because we are called to be a *people* of prayer. Acts 2:42 describes the life of the early Church: "They were continually devoting themselves to the apostles' teaching and to fellowship, to the breaking of bread and to prayer." Acts 12:5 says, "So Peter was kept in the prison, but prayer for him was being made fervently by the church to God." An angel came and released him. Prayer was being made not by an elite group of intercessors but by the Church. Addressing the whole church at Ephesus and not a special group of intercessors, Paul wrote:

> With all prayer and petition pray at all times in the Spirit, and with this in view, be on the alert with all perseverance and petition for all the saints, and pray on my behalf, that utterance may be given to me in the opening of my mouth, to make known with boldness the mystery of the gospel, for which I am an ambassador in chains; that in proclaiming it I may speak boldly, as I ought to speak.
>
> Ephesians 6:18–20

Authority to pray effectively lies with the Body of Christ whose very lifeblood is prayer, rather than with an elite group.

The third problem with the "intercessor" delusion is that it takes something essential away from those who do not bear that designation. I have watched those who were told, "You are not an intercessor," or who assumed, "I am not an inter-cessor," simply stop praying for issues beyond themselves. They felt diminished and withdrew. Divisions developed in the church as a result. I take responsibility for allowing this to happen in my own congregation. In the end I asked forgiveness from our people and then took responsibility for repairing the damage. The prophetic task is to enable and strengthen a church, not to contribute to division and certainly not to diminish anyone in a calling God lays upon every believer.

Prayer Cover

Prayer cover has sprung up in recent years as another un-biblical term that sounds logical but when misused serves to exalt our fleshly sense of importance. We speak of ministries as needing "prayer cover," and some refer to themselves as "prayer cover" as if it were the people or the prayers them-selves that protect us and prosper our ministries. Wrong! Again we inflate ourselves at Jesus' expense, and allow our-selves to become puffed up in our own sense of importance, place and position. Jesus alone is our rock and our salvation. He sovereignly and graciously chooses to enlist us in praying for the progress and protection of ministries. In doing so, He allows us to participate with Him in what He is doing because He loves us and loves to be in relationship with us.

Do not misunderstand. I regard prayer for my own min-istry to be essential and would never engage in any significant endeavor without brothers and sisters praying with me. But nowhere do the Scriptures credit "prayer cover" in the way I hear it described today. Paul credits prayer as having an effect on the progress of his ministry in 2 Corinthians 1:11: "You also [are] joining in helping us through your prayers, so that thanks may be given by many persons on our behalf for the favor bestowed on us through the prayers of many." But this kind of affirmation stops well short of what we have made it today. "Helping" is not the same as "covering."

Peter was set free from prison while the saints were praying (see Acts 12:5), but by contrast Paul and Silas had no such "prayer cover" when they were imprisoned and locked in the stocks after being beaten with rods. They were simply worshiping on their own when the earthquake came and their chains fell off (see Acts 16:25–26). What is more, the biblical account employs no language of cause and effect between their acts of worship and their miraculous deliverance.

I love to be supported in prayer when I am engaged in ministry, and I love it that my overall ministry is being prayed for every hour of the day. But I refuse to attach a magical significance to it that credits people with my protection rather than the hand of Jesus, my rock and my salvation.

Prophetic Declarations

It has become a fashionable thing in prophetic and charismatic circles to make "prophetic declarations." The idea behind a prophetic declaration is that by declaring aloud that something will happen, we somehow cause it to come to pass. With qualifications, I agree with this principle. Isaiah 55:11 says, "So will My word be which goes forth from My mouth; it will not return to Me empty, without accomplishing what I desire, and without succeeding in the matter for which I sent it."

It can be so easy, however, to forget where the word must originate. In our immaturity and fleshly need to feel powerful, we can overlook the necessity for such declarations to have their true source in God. His word, not ours, creates reality and accomplishes the purposes of heaven. Anything else is foolish posturing. The prophet has no authority in himself or herself. All authority in heaven and on earth is given to Jesus. Apart from Him we stand empty.

We must never therefore merely determine what we want to see happen, no matter how good, loving or appealing it might seem, and then prophetically declare it as if to make it come to pass. This would be presumption. Like Jesus, if the Father is speaking, then we speak. If He is silent, then we must be silent.

The early years with the church I now pastor were difficult, to say the least. Our congregation was born under a hail of curses and lies directed at us from outside. Internally, we gathered an initial crop of horribly wounded and broken people. They ripped and tore at one another with criticism and suspicion, demanding unreasonable levels of counsel and care and stirring up strife when we failed to deliver at the level of their demand. Nothing we did was ever enough. It was awful.

After years of prayer, one night during a time of intercession I heard the Lord speak and knew that I was to repeat His words aloud as what some would call a "prophetic declaration." The word I heard was, "The reign of terror is ended." In actual experience it was not quite over, but the word of the Lord—when it is truly His word—never returns empty without accomplishing what He desires. I spoke this in the Lord's name on more than one occasion over a period of time, declaring what was yet to come as if it were a present reality because its coming was certain. As time passed, power flowed, God moved according to His word and our congregation experienced a radical transformation, which I can summarize by saying that church is fun again!

Prophetic declarations proclaim what is to be as if it already is. In the proclaiming, power goes forth to accomplish the purposes of God, but the strong qualifier is that such words must indeed be the words of God rather than mere expressions of the hopes, dreams and desires of men and women.

Paul made a prophetic declaration in Acts 13 when Elymas the magician opposed him before the proconsul on the island of Paphos:

> But Saul, who was also known as Paul, filled with the Holy Spirit, fixed his gaze on him, and said, "You who are full of all deceit and fraud, you son of the devil, you enemy of all righteousness, will you not cease to make crooked the straight ways of the Lord? Now, *behold, the hand of the Lord is upon you, and you will be blind and not see the sun for a time.*" And immediately a mist and a darkness fell upon him, and he went about seeking those who would lead him by the hand.
>
> verses 9–11, emphasis mine

Paul saw or heard what God wanted done and spoke it prophetically. Because he spoke God's own word, it came to pass. Neither the words nor the authority behind them originated in Paul but, rather, in the Lord.

The best precedents for prophetic declaration are, of course, Jesus' own. Remember that He spoke only what He heard His Father speaking. Let's look at two examples.

In Matthew 8, the centurion came to Jesus seeking healing for a beloved servant lying paralyzed at home. Verse 13 says, "And Jesus said to the centurion, 'Go; it shall be done for you as you have believed.' And the servant was healed that very moment."

In Matthew 9:22, Jesus turned to the woman with the twelve-year flow of blood and said, "'Daughter, take courage; your faith has made you well.' At once the woman was made well." In both of these cases, Jesus neither issued a command nor prayed. He heard from His Father and made a simple and direct declaration of what would become reality.

By Jesus' own testimony, I have no trouble understanding that had He declared anything at all on His own authority, nothing would have happened. In the Church today, prophetic declarations work not on the authority of the prophet but on the authority of God who speaks His own will *through* the prophet. This again underscores the need for prophetic people to seek true intimacy with God in order to hear the content of His will.

The Hidden Role of the Prophet

Prophetic people often falsely assume that they must stand in the public eye, that prophetic ministry is about speaking before crowds of people and being known. This is an easy conclusion to draw, given the fact that most of the prophets we see named in Scripture did occupy such positions.

But we must take a deeper look. After Samuel anointed Saul as king, he told him to go to the hill of God where there was a Philistine garrison and "meet a group of prophets coming down from the high place with harp, tambourine, flute, and a lyre before them, and they will be prophesying" (1 Samuel 10:5). Here we see a group of prophets worshiping near the city, but to whom were they prophesying? What was the content? If prophetic ministry is about being heard and known, why do we read not a single word of what any of them had to say?

In 1 Samuel 19, Saul had descended into jealous paranoid madness and sent men to seize David, but they encountered a company of prophets prophesying under Samuel's supervision and were so overcome by the Spirit of God that they, too, began to prophesy. Three times this happened until finally Saul himself came and the Spirit of God overwhelmed him, as well, so that he prophesied! David was delivered from Saul's attack. But once again, we know nothing about these prophets, who they were or what they said. It further appears that they prophesied not publicly but only within their own group. Even if they did prophesy publicly, it seems apparent that both their identities and the content of their prophesying remained hidden. They were a nameless and faceless company.

In the days of Elijah we know that there were many prophets. In 1 Kings 18, Obadiah, who had charge of the household of King Ahab, hid one hundred of them in caves to protect them from Jezebel's wrath. Again we know nothing of their names or words. We hear only of Elijah and Obadiah by name and read only the words those two spoke, until Elisha emerges as Elijah's successor.

The short point is that few prophets stood out and attracted public attention. The others apparently labored mostly in obscurity and hiddenness except when they emerged as a group, which would constitute a form of anonymity in numbers.

The New Testament list is short, as previously noted. We read of the daughters of Philip the evangelist (see Acts 21:8–9), Judas and Silas (see Acts 15:32), Agabus (see Acts 11:27–28 and 21:10), Anna (see Luke 2:36), anonymous prophets mentioned in 1 Corinthians 14:2 and John the

Baptist. None of their words are recorded for us except two prophecies through Agabus and the message of John the Baptist preparing the way for Jesus. In Luke 2 Simeon spoke prophetically to Mary and Joseph concerning Jesus and His destiny, but Luke does not specifically identify him as a prophet. No books and not a single miracle are attributed to any New Testament prophet.

Clearly, being prophetic is no ticket to public recognition. The public platform seems to be a rare thing for the prophetic person. In fact, "stage hunger" indicates immaturity in a prophetically gifted person and leads directly to delusion and harm.

It would be a fair conclusion, then, to assume that prophetic ministry happens mostly in the hiddenness of intercession and that public recognition and prominence would be the exception and not the rule for modern-day prophetic people. Even when granted the platform and/or widespread recognition, mature prophetic people prefer hidden intimacy with God to the seductive influence of the adulation of the masses. This preference flows from humility and holy fear. The Lord's prophet must be filled with zeal for God but void of ambition and the need for visibility. "When there are many words, transgression is unavoidable, but he who restrains his lips is wise" (Proverbs 10:19). My seasoned prophetic father says that we need to get over the idea that prophecy is all about "blabbing." Allergy to the microphone is a good thing.

6

THE OFFICE OF PROPHET

Any member of the Body of Christ can prophesy. Joel said it in Joel 2:28: "Your sons and daughters will prophesy." The apostle Paul wrote it in 1 Corinthians 14:

> Pursue love, yet desire earnestly spiritual gifts, but especially that you may prophesy. . . . Now I wish that you all spoke in tongues, but even more that you would prophesy. . . . But if all prophesy, and an unbeliever or an ungifted man enters, he is convicted by all, he is called to account by all; the secrets of his heart are disclosed; and so he will fall on his face and worship God, declaring that God is certainly among you.
>
> 1 Corinthians 14:1, 5, 24–25

All believers may therefore prophesy, and Paul encouraged them to do so. For this reason, many of us may exercise the gift of prophecy from time to time to greater or lesser degrees. Some may even prophesy consistently enough to be called "prophetic."

The office of prophet, however, differs from the momentary gifting available to the average believer and even from the kind of frequency of prophetic ministry that qualifies one as "prophetic." Prophetic officeholders are a rare breed. While Paul encouraged all to seek to prophesy, only those few previously listed—together with those nameless ones identified as prophets in 1 Corinthians 14:2 and John the Baptist—are recognized as prophets in the New Testament. A short list indeed!

While any of us can prophesy from time to time "for the common good" (1 Corinthians 12:7) as the Lord distributes "to each one individually" (12:11) according to the need of the moment, the prophetic officeholder bears the calling as the definition of his or her being. True prophets live it day in and day out, sensing at all times the weight of God's calling and presence. Every bit of life, even ordinary events, can take on prophetic overtones.

Where normal people see simply a glorious sunset, for instance, the prophet might discern a message for the times in the symbolism of the colors. Jeremiah saw the rod of an almond tree. Most people would have seen only a nut tree about to blossom—a common enough thing in agrarian Israel—but in that moment Jeremiah understood it as a symbolic message from God concerning the budding fulfillment of the Lord's word (see Jeremiah 1:11–12). Normal people might observe seven men crossing the street together, but for the prophet the number might hold symbolic meaning as a veiled message from God that the fullness of God's people are about to cross over into the promise.

My daughter Charity lost three babies after the birth of her first. The third miscarriage was a tubal pregnancy that burst, causing a hemorrhage that nearly killed her. Heartbroken and grieved, she cried out to the Lord to give her back what had been taken. She wanted to bear twins. Not long afterward, in a prayer meeting at our church, God told me clearly that Charity would conceive and that her pregnancy would prophetically signal the beginning of the end of barrenness for our church. Within a month or two, she did, in fact, become pregnant. And it was twins! I took it as the sign the Lord had promised. She took it personally, as she should have.

One difficult year in our church I found myself questioning my call to Denver. In prayer the Lord responded by telling me, "Count the sevens. It is a year of sevens for you." I knew that seven symbolizes fullness in Scripture, so I understood what He might be trying to show me. In the end, I compiled three pages of sevens that had come together in my life that year. Let me give you just a few examples: The number of our street address upon moving to Denver was 10321. The numbers added up to seven. That year we moved to a new townhouse in a different neighborhood. The address was 1222. Again a seven! I had purchased the seventh guitar I had owned since I began playing as a teenager. My car was the seventh I had owned since beginning my adult life. That year I released my seventh music CD. It was our seventh year in the city of Denver. Seven family members lived in Denver with me. The Lord even told me that the Denver Broncos would win the Super Bowl that year by a margin of seven. I feared that I might have heard wrong until they scored a touchdown in the last two minutes of the game and then made the extra point to win by seven. I got the message. I am still in Denver.

Not all prophets think in such symbolic terms or interpret ordinary events in such unique ways—the wise among us do so only when the Lord tells us to—but every prophet I know has a different way of perceiving the world than the average believer does. The calling is all-consuming.

Prophetic Presence

A prophetic officeholder carries an air of anointing, authority and presence that validates itself in the eyes of the people. Prophetic people who prophesy only occasionally experience this kind of authority and validation on a momentary basis as people respond to the word given. But prophetic officeholders carry it with them all the time. They may not be conscious of carrying that air of authority, but people around them feel it even when they do not.

This air of authority or presence can be intimidating to others, although it need not be when it is shielded in the mature. My father, for instance, is a widely recognized prophetic voice in the Body of Christ today. I have often said that I married the first woman who could look him directly in the eye. Before I met Beth, the penetrating nature of his gift wilted more than a few of the girls I brought home. He did not mean to affect them that way—not consciously anyway. Whether or not he wanted it to, the authority of his gift came through, and where prospective brides for me were concerned, I doubt he worked very hard at shielding himself!

People often fear that kind of presence. A true prophet can fill a room without ever saying a word, and it can sometimes cause people who are not so gifted to feel they are being restrained or stifled. This can be made worse if the rejection issues so common among prophetic people have not been healed. Insecurity and rejection form a fertile seedbed for domination and control mechanisms that twist and misuse the anointing. Mature and seasoned prophets have learned to shepherd God's people, to draw them out and into their own gifts. In humility they know when and how to hold back or shield prophetic presence so as to make room for others to blossom and grow.

Too often those who are still immature and unbroken revel in their own gifting and authority at the expense of the edification of others and therefore cause much unnecessary wounding and offense. They not only do not know when to shut their mouths, but they also feel exhilarated in their domination of meetings and encounters with others. This is one of the places where many immature prophetic people create offense with pastors and other leadership.

Joseph suffered from this kind of immaturity before his brothers grew tired of his arrogant attitude and sold him into slavery (see Genesis 37). He would have been wiser to keep his dreams and his gifting to himself for his brothers' sakes until maturity and seasoning taught him wisdom. As it was, he had to learn that wisdom the hard way in slavery and then in prison in Egypt. Immature prophets often earn the rejection they experience.

Sometimes God moves and speaks, on the other hand, in ways that make it impossible to hide prophetic presence. I suspect that Samuel quite consciously allowed the authority of his office to flow out from him when he confronted King Saul with his disobedience in offering a sacrifice before Samuel's return (see 1 Samuel 13). And I am sure Elijah did not do much to mask his anointing when he slew the 450 prophets of Baal (see 1 Kings 18).

Whether prophetic presence is projected validly under the anointing or foolishly through the immature, it can draw rejection from those threatened by it. It can cause others to feel small and insignificant. Even when pride is absent and humility has become an established element of character, the authority radiating from a prophet can elicit accusations of arrogance. Aaron and Miriam, Moses' closest and most trusted associates, succumbed to this when they accused Moses, "Has the LORD indeed spoken only through Moses? Has He not spoken through us as well?" (Numbers 12:2).

Having said this much, I would caution budding prophetic officeholders concerning the vast difference between being persecuted for genuine anointing, as were Jeremiah and Moses, and being persecuted for being obnoxious, foolish and insensitive, as was Joseph. One is holy. The other is not. I have been personally rejected and wounded for both causes. I would obviously prefer to be attacked for the real thing rather than for my lingering character flaws, but I know none of us will ever be entirely immune to the need for rebuke where character flaws are concerned.

While writing this chapter, the Lord prompted me to ponder Zechariah 13, a passage with which I have always struggled. Whether or not we fully understand what it meant and how it applied in its historical context, the Lord's word to me was that a time like this will come for the Church today.

> "In that day a fountain will be opened for the house of David and for the inhabitants of Jerusalem, for sin and for impurity. It will come about in that day," declares the LORD of hosts, "that I will cut off the names of the idols from the land, and they will no longer be remembered; and I will also remove the prophets and the unclean spirit from the land. And if anyone still prophesies, then his father and mother who gave birth to him will say to him, 'You shall not live, for you have spoken falsely in the name of the LORD'; and his father and mother who gave birth to him will pierce him through when he prophesies. Also it will come about in that day that the prophets will each be ashamed of his vision when he prophesies, and they will not put on a hairy robe in order to deceive; but he will say, 'I am not a prophet; I am a tiller of the ground, for a man sold me as a slave in my youth.' And one will say to him, 'What are these wounds between your arms?' Then

he will say, 'Those with which I was wounded in the house
of my friends.' Awake, O sword, against My Shepherd, and
against the man, My Associate," declares the LORD of hosts.
"Strike the Shepherd that the sheep may be scattered; and I
will turn My hand against the little ones. It will come about
in all the land," declares the LORD, "that two parts in it will
be cut off and perish; but the third will be left in it. And I
will bring the third part through the fire, refine them as silver
is refined, and test them as gold is tested. They will call on
My name, and I will answer them; I will say, 'They are My
people,' and they will say, 'The LORD is my God.'"

Zechariah 13:1–9

The word of application the Lord gave me is this: *A time
is yet coming for the disciplining and cleansing of the prophets
and the shepherds, a time when the unclean spirit is removed
from among the people and from the hearts of the prophets and
the shepherds. Humility will take hold and no longer will those
who think themselves prophetic promote themselves. Rather than
claim, "I am a prophet," prophetic people will stand in humbler
places, seeing themselves as mere human beings like anyone
else. They will no longer be so eager to speak everything they
see or hear or dream but will be content not to be noticed and
to keep their visions to themselves if need be. This will coincide
with a movement of purification and holiness among the Body
of Christ at large—a time of fiery testing and purging in order
that the genuine might emerge bearing the marks of Christ in
spirit and in character.*

Self-Validating Authority

The true prophet never needs to sell him- or herself. As
maturity develops and repentance for inner strongholds of
rejection takes effect so that healing comes, he or she never

needs or craves recognition. Self-promoters are dangerous. As a pastor who has been burned I instinctively recoil whenever anyone comes to me reciting his prophetic credentials and seeking recognition. I would rather he show me in humility than tell me in order to sell me.

In the current climate of imbalance where sanctified psychic reading and personal prophecies comprise the dominant prophetic model, too many have received words from the platform at some conference or ministry school exalting them as prophets when they are not. When they return home, they begin to sell themselves to others, as if to convince others of their office on the strength of the word of the famous one who spoke the word over them. When the anticipated recognition or desired platform fails to materialize, offense is often taken, and wounded pastoral leadership takes a cautious step backward.

In the Eyes of the Body of Christ

When the Body of Christ recognizes someone as a prophetic officeholder, then he or she holds the office. Not before. Prophetic authority validates itself in the eyes of others because of the love it conveys, the truth it brings and the power it releases for the edification of the Body of Christ. One is not a prophet because he or she claims to be or because he or she feels called to be. One is a prophet because the Body of Christ recognizes the anointing based on fruit. This was true of each and every prophet in Scripture. In fact, at least one of them, Amos, denied that he was a prophet despite the fact that his inclusion in the canon secures his place as one.

Amos replied to Amaziah, "I am not a prophet, nor am I the son of a prophet; for I am a herdsman and a grower of sycamore figs. But the LORD took me from following the flock and the LORD said to me, 'Go prophesy to My people Israel.'"

Amos 7:14–15

In humility he himself denied his office, but the people of Israel validated it!

When a true prophet ministers to me and his or her innate authority touches me, I feel transparent. Something in me crumbles and I am plucked up and planted, torn down and built up (see Jeremiah 1:10).

In 1988 I attended a meeting of pastors in Seattle at which John Paul Jackson ministered. One at a time John Paul fixed his gaze on each of the pastors gathered there—except me, or so I thought—and prophesied into their lives. Accustomed to being overlooked and left out, I therefore assumed he had finished when he stopped suddenly and fell silent. After some time had passed, he pointed a single finger in my direction without ever looking up and began to speak. He told me that there was a room reserved for me called "The Mystical Experiences of God." He said that I had placed my hand on the door handle but had never opened it. He indicated that this was not to my discredit. I had never opened it because I thought that my father's calling lay inside. He told me that my father's calling did not lie inside. Mine did. He said that this room reserved for me was higher than my father's, that my vision would be clear because my father had fought through the fog before me and prepared the way. I was completely undone. I had struggled through my father's learning years of imbalance when there were no mentors to make things easier. Somewhere in my heart, even as a child, I had determined not to go the way of imbalance, and I had shut down the mystical prophetic side of my own calling.

After receiving John Paul's word, I wandered around in a fog for two or three days, plucked up and planted, torn down and built up. The prophetic word releases power to accomplish the will of God. This contributes to credibility and an air of prophetic presence. When a true prophet ministers, you sense the power of it as the presence of God comes in a wonderfully disconcerting, yet restful, way.

Two years later an angel visited me in a dream to tell me to go to Denver. The prophecy began to unfold, and every year from that time until now I have experienced a deeper realization of what John Paul prophesied that day.

In April 2005 my father and I ministered together in a large interracial church in the London, England, metroplex. On the final night we were asked to prophesy over the leadership of the church as they lined up on the platform. I recall little of what I said to them as the Holy Spirit filled me, but I do recall that it had to do with the closure of a season of turmoil and dishonor of leadership and the beginning of a new season that would be·a time of blessing, increase and influence in the city. I remember saying that the Lord had closed the door on that old season and that it would not come again. I was unaware that only one week earlier a pastoral staff member had left the church after an extended period of conflict, dishonor and rebellion that had defiled many in the congregation. Afterward, leadership at the meeting declared, "These men are prophets!"—a title I remain uncomfortable with. I wanted to crawl under a chair and hide. But this illustrates the point that prophetic authority validates itself. Reports later came to us of new freedom and prophetic power in the worship at that church.

Two cautions bear repeating here. First, no matter what ministry you find yourself successfully engaged in, never believe your own press. Obedience has value. Personal praise has none. Delusions or even justifiable assumptions of personal grandeur lead directly to shipwreck. Second, when the seventy disciples returned from their missionary journey rejoicing that the demons were subject to them in Jesus' name, He told them, "Nevertheless do not rejoice in this, that the spirits are subject to you, but rejoice that your names are recorded in heaven" (Luke 10:20). Never allow yourself to be carried away by the thrill of the power and gifting given to you. Rejoice instead that you are simply and always a mere sinner saved by grace. Therein lies the humility that forms the antidote for delusions of grandeur.

Substance and Specificity

No biblical prophet—Old or New Testament—ever spoke in pleasant generalities. Their words held substance, which meant that they carried life-confronting, life-changing weight. And they spoke with "specificity," meaning that their words had an edge to them, containing revelatory specifics that anchored them in measurable reality and provided clear directions for action, healing and restoration.

In the book of Acts, Agabus prophesied with substance and specificity concerning famine to come and the imprisonment of Paul. Jeremiah outlined Israel's sin, describing in detail the destruction to come and prescribing repentance as the remedy, if Israel would only respond. There was weight and meat to what he had to say in the Lord's name.

In recent years the Lord has commanded me never to preside over a wedding or funeral without including a prophetic word for the people involved. During the funeral of Jenna's mother, Marilyn (not their real names), who passed away after a lengthy period of deterioration, I gave a prophetic word for the family as part of the pastoral prayer. The word was good, but the real impact came at the end as I tried to focus on the benediction. During the final song before the benediction, I kept hearing, "Tell Marilyn she didn't fail." I pushed it away, not wanting to deal with the theological implications of what it seemed I was being asked to do. It would not go away. In fact, it kept growing louder the more I tried to ignore it. So I stopped in the middle of the benediction and addressed the family, "Forgive me if I'm wrong, but I have to say this because I believe I'm hearing it from God. 'Marilyn! You didn't fail! Marilyn! You didn't fail!'"

Immediately after the benediction, I knelt before Jenna and said, "I hope that was okay, because if it wasn't, I'm a real jerk." Through tear-filled eyes she told me, "As my mother was dying on her last day, she kept saying, 'I failed you.'" At the reception that followed the service, people lined up to thank me for that word. It gave me the opportunity to speak the reality of Jesus to a number of folks who did not know Him. Substance and specificity.

When I perform a wedding, I include a prophetic word in the prayer of pastoral blessing. I pray about it beforehand and write down what I receive, partly because I want to be careful, but also so the couple will have it in writing for future reference. In that context I once prophesied over a couple as they renewed their vows in a full wedding ceremony after a separation precipitated by adultery. God said to tell them that a severe testing would come soon and that when it came it would be crucial that they cling to what they had recently learned from the Lord in order to survive it. If they would do that, the experience would strengthen them immeasurably as a couple.

Within three weeks the mother of the infant child conceived through the husband's adultery began to cause trouble over the issue of child visitation and support. Rather than cling to the Lord, John (not his real name) turned to alcohol and in his drunkenness did things that landed him in jail. Unfortunately he failed to heed the prophetic word, but the word itself had substance and specificity. To their credit, that couple later turned it all around and ended up more solid than they had been before. God is indeed merciful!

A 42-year-old mother died of congestive heart failure. She was a believer in Jesus but had not been involved in church for many years, although her family and friends knew of her faith and regarded her as a loving person. Her family, good people, had followed her lead and remained unchurched. I was delighted when they asked me to preside over the funeral, and as per my instructions, I listened for the prophetic word.

Toward the end of the service, again as I contemplated the benediction, I began to see a mental vision of this mother standing in heaven, arms held wide, face filled with rapturous wonder, crying out, "I missed it! There is so much more!" I struggled with whether to speak the vision aloud or not, but as I kept it to myself, the pressure only grew until I finally introduced it the way I usually do. "If I'm wrong, please forgive me, but this is what I believe I'm seeing." And I described the vision. Tears began to flow.

Afterward four or five people approached me to express their thanks and to say they were going to rejoin the Body of Christ in a church near them. An equal number told me I would see them in my own church. They felt the touch of God that day. This is substance and specificity that produces the fruit of plucking up and planting, tearing down and building up!

Vaporous words such as "Behold! God is doing something new! Get ready!" may be true—and I have heard and read that one literally every year of my adult life. But they lack any kind of substance, specificity or real revelatory content.

Unfortunately most of what passes as prophetic in churches today sounds a lot like that. It is "nice" but comes up short on substance and genuine revelation.

After Hurricane Katrina struck the U.S. Gulf Coast, a number of us with prophetic ministries received words that the disasters had not ended but that they would spread north in a variety of forms from fire to earthquake. A national movement of prayer and repentance could mitigate this, but it would certainly come. Hurricane Rita followed on the heels of Katrina. Storms devastated areas of California and triggered mudslides that destroyed many homes. In the succeeding months huge fires raged across Oklahoma, destroying thousands of acres and hundreds of homes. There were huge fires in southern Colorado. Fires burned 445,000 acres in Texas. Later, on March 13, 2006, the headline on CNN.com read, "Texas Wildfires Scorch 600,000 Acres, Kill 7." The fires continued to burn out of control, fanned by high winds. The same day saw deadly tornadoes in Missouri and Illinois. One in Missouri was a half-mile wide! So many tornadoes caused so much devastation that later the Missouri governor declared the state a disaster area. These are just a few examples. More will yet come. Here was revelatory power, calling God's people to prayer with substance and specificity.

Prophetic officeholders wrestle with these issues. The need for substance and specificity forms part of the burden the prophet carries. The pressure of that need can contribute to an air of heaviness and the overserious natures of some prophetic people.

Signs of a True Prophet

So how can the Church differentiate between a prophetic person and a true prophet? The ministries of true prophets will be characterized by four things: fulfillment, creative edification, perceptive insight and restoration and healing.

Fulfillment

Fulfillment comes in two forms. First, if the word is predictive, then we must look for the realization of the prediction. Deuteronomy 18:22 bears repeating here: "When a prophet speaks in the name of the LORD, if the thing does not come about or come true, that is the thing which the LORD has not spoken. The prophet has spoken it presumptuously; you shall not be afraid of him."

Second, if the word is of the Jeremiah 1:10 variety—"to pluck up and to break down, to destroy and to overthrow, to build and to plant"—then fulfillment means that the word has accomplished the purpose for which it was sent. It will tear down what is not of God and release power to set the things of God in motion. Isaiah 55:11 says, "So will My word be which goes forth from My mouth; it will not return to Me empty, without accomplishing what I desire, and without succeeding in the matter for which I sent it."

One essential mark of the office of prophet is that his or her words consistently come to pass and produce the effect God intended, although I do not believe the New Testament requires 100 percent accuracy. Agabus did not have it quite right when he prophesied Paul's arrest, for instance. The Romans bound him, not the Jews as Agabus expected (see Acts 21:11). The original apostles clearly expected that Jesus would return within their lifetimes. The actual events they prophesied will yet come to pass because the Word of God remains true, but the timeline in their own hearts was skewed. Consistency in fulfillment and in effect nevertheless remains an essential evidence of prophetic office.

Creative Edification

When a prophet anointed an Old Testament king, something real happened. The anointing released power that set the course of the anointed one's life. First Corinthians 14:4–5 describes the same dynamic:

> One who speaks in a tongue edifies himself; but one who prophesies edifies the church. Now I wish that you all spoke in tongues, but even more that you would prophesy; and greater is one who prophesies than one who speaks in tongues, unless he interprets, so that the church may receive edifying.

Good prophecy releases power that sets the course of lives and fellowships. All of us, prophetic or not, have been called to build up the Body of Christ. The prophetic word, however, does so uniquely and powerfully.

Let us look once again at 1 Corinthians 14:3: "But one who prophesies speaks to men for edification and exhortation and consolation." Read this in the light of what has been said concerning the authority of a true prophet. Paraphrased, the verse says that the prophetic word builds up, then strongly motivates the one built up to go and do something with what has been given, and then settles (consoles) the individual or the Body of Christ in the prophetic word and in the forms of preparatory tribulation that may lead up to it.

Anyone who prophesies a true word can have this effect on others, but the prophetic officeholder has this effect consistently. He or she lives for this and *knows* that he or she lives for this. Where a true prophet walks, life blooms.

Perceptive Insight

I have already spoken to the issue of sanctified psychic reading. Perceptive insight is much like this but goes well beyond it. Consider Jesus' encounter with the woman at the well in John 4. A contemporary psychic reader passing as a prophet might have said to her, "God shows me that you have been married before and that you have had a number of sexual partners." That would be an easy set of generalizations. Almost anyone with a fully alive human spirit could have picked up that much just by sensing the condition of this woman's soul.

Jesus, however, is the prototypical prophet (and much more, of course). He said to her, "You have had five husbands, and the one whom you now have is not your husband; this you have said truly" (verse 18). He perceived not just that she had been married before, but specifically that she had been married five times, and not just that she had led an immoral life in the past, but that she was currently engaged in an illicit relationship. The prophetic officeholder therefore perceives not in generalities, but incisively and with substance and specificity.

A visiting missionary attended a prayer meeting in which I participated. At the end of the meeting we blessed her for her next endeavor. She had testified earlier regarding some serious health problems of which the Lord had healed her. As we prayed, I "saw" that there was a lingering health threat of some kind hovering over her at her back. Feeling a bit insecure, I spoke aloud only a portion of what I had seen, leaving out the part about seeing it at her back. I prayed for healing. Afterward a friend of hers told me that she had a sore or lesion of some kind on her back that would not heal without serious plastic surgery. How much was mere sanctified psychic reading and how much was prophetic substance and specificity? I wish I knew. I would like to think it was more, but my true concern is only that she felt herself ministered to and that she received an assurance that God intended to do something about her problem.

Restoration and Healing

In 1 Kings 17 Elijah came to the widow of Zarephath in a time of famine seeking a meal. Miraculously, God multiplied the last of her food to feed Elijah, the widow and her son throughout the time of famine. Later, however, the son died. Verses 21–22 describes how Elijah prayed for this young man:

> Then he stretched himself upon the child three times, and called to the LORD and said, "O LORD my God, I pray You, let this child's life return to him." The LORD heard the voice of Elijah, and the life of the child returned to him and he revived.

In 2 Kings 4 Elisha received an appeal from a widow of one of the prophets who had fallen on difficult economic times. Elisha instructed her to gather vessels for oil and pour into them what oil she had. The oil never stopped until all were filled. The sale of the oil carried her and her children through the difficulties.

Not all healers are prophets, but all prophets must be healers and restorers. This can manifest in the healing of bodies, as in 1 Kings when Elijah prayed for the widow's son to be raised from the dead. Or it can be restoration of the sort that the widow in 2 Kings 4 experienced. It also can be healing of the heart or the healing of reconciliation between individuals and people groups.

Many prophets with whom I have been acquainted began their ministries as counselors. My father started that way and now invests himself primarily in reconciliation ministry between people groups. Early in his ministry John Paul Jackson had a counseling ministry. He still writes healing books.

True prophets follow their Lord as peacemakers. They bring healing, not prophetic lacerations disguised as confrontation in love. Even in confrontation, true prophets exhibit a tenderness and pleading in love that points toward healing. God is love. His true prophets reflect His true nature.

PART 2

HEARING GOD

7

MEDITATION

Clearly, prophetic people hear from God for others and for the Body of Christ. The single most important key to hearing from God is intimacy with Him, and the most important key to intimacy is meditation. Meditation is our own Christian gift of spirituality. Prophetic people must master it or increase the risk of hearing from sources other than God.

It is a gift, however, that has been stolen and twisted by others. Most Christians hold little interest in meditation—in part because of a misdirected reaction to Hindus and New Agers, who have stolen something that rightly belongs to us. The Church seems to have a bad habit of abandoning good things to the enemy just because the enemy has adopted and twisted them, assuming falsely that if the enemy does something, then we cannot. But the enemy of our souls is not a creator and can seldom be credited with originating anything. He can only steal from us what God has made and then twist and distort it. Meditation is like that. Some of what you are about to read may sound like the practices of New Agers and other cults, but our own Book teaches about meditation, and it is time for us to reclaim it and do it right.

Another influence that has made meditation a forgotten practice is our secular culture of action and entertainment. We do not know how to be still. In a world filled with a great deal more noise than we realize, silence makes us uncomfortable. During the winter of 2005–2006 my home was without power for twelve hours. The silence was deafening. There was no motor driving the refrigerator, no humming of the furnace fan or sound of rushing air, no pumps rumbling quietly under the fish tank and no television. My wife and I hardly knew what to do with ourselves. We need noise! And we had not realized how much there was.

Worse, when presented with the opportunity to be still, we had not a clue what to do. Life in the modern world moves at a tremendous pace, and we have become attuned to it. Our minds and hearts pulse to the rhythm of constant stimulation and entertainment. Meditation surrenders all that, at least for a time, in order to hear the voice of God who often speaks in whispers still and small, as if to assert His unwillingness to compete actively with the noise in the world around us.

More is said about meditation in the Old Testament than in the New Testament, which is another reason Christians tend to neglect the practice. The New Testament was not written as a book of meditations but rather as an account of actions, events and exhortations. It records the *deeds* of Jesus and points out the Old Testament underpinnings for its teachings, taking for granted the authority and instruction deposited there that had already been handed down through the ages. It contains the *Acts* of the apostles, rather than an account of their prayer life.

Much of the foundation for our spirituality is therefore laid in the Old Testament, which every one of the New Testament writers regarded as the Word of God still in force. Second Timothy 3:16–17 teaches, "All Scripture is inspired by God and profitable for teaching, for reproof, for correction, for training in righteousness; so that the man of God may be adequate, equipped for every good work." The New Testament had yet to be written. Paul spoke of the only Scripture he knew—the Old Testament.

Finally, we must understand that meditation is not prayer in the purest sense. In prayer we actively engage ourselves in a conversation with God. In meditation we place ourselves in a passive, receiving mode. As we enter into a state of peace and rest in Him, the flow moves from God to us. He speaks, and we receive His words.

Sound

Primarily two Hebrew words are translated as *meditation*. The first, *hagah*, refers to a "low sound, such as the moaning of a dove or the growling of a lion over its prey; a muttering or a sighing." Meditation is therefore associated with inarticulate sounds that resonate in the throat and in the soul of the one meditating.

In Joshua 1:8 God gave this instruction:

"This book of the law shall not depart from your mouth, but you shall meditate [*hagah*] on it day and night, so that you may be careful to do according to all that is written in it; for then you will make your way prosperous, and then you will have success."

Joshua received a command to meditate on the law day and night in order to do all that is in it. God promised power for success in taking the Promised Land as a result. Like Joshua, therefore, we must receive God's law into our hearts and allow it to resonate there as if it were a sound. We must at least figuratively vibrate with it as if it were a penetrating frequency pulsing through us until it becomes part of us. Then we will begin to do what the law requires because it will be a vibrant part of us, expressing itself without forethought or effort. In this kind of inner environment, God can speak and we can hear.

I suspect this was what the apostle Paul had in mind in the New Testament book of Romans when he wrote, "In the same way the Spirit also helps our weakness; for we do not know how to pray as we should, but the Spirit Himself intercedes for us with groanings too deep for words" (8:26). I am certain Paul wrote about what happens when we deeply focus on the Holy Spirit and let Him fill us in meditation.

The key concept in *hagah* is *sound*. In Bible times, people prayed out loud rather than quietly in the heart as has become our practice in the modern Western world. They made an audible sound!

I find it interesting that when a group of people prays aloud together in tongues it creates a low rumbling that is conducive to meditation. I recommend praying much in tongues—not in a way that focuses on a goal or purpose but passively, restfully and aloud. Praying aloud in tongues incorporates sound, but it is a sound with content—"tongues of men and of angels" (1 Corinthians 13:1). Even better, because it is a form of content that bypasses our conscious understanding, it involves no active mental process or effort of the flesh.

Over the last few years music—sound—for meditating has become extremely popular among Christians. We have a recording studio in our church where we record our original worship music. Our CDs for meditating and soaking in the presence of the Lord outsell our other albums by a margin of ten to one, and other Christian musicians are experiencing the same phenomenon. This speaks of a growing hunger among God's people to find and enter His presence.

Sound carries a unique capacity to inspire emotions in us. The right kind of sound can lead us into meditative peace and so prepare us to receive the word of the Lord. God is calling us to hear Him more accurately for these crucial times. To accomplish this, we must learn to come to the quiet place in meditation. In meditation, therefore, we seek to be still and to allow the sound we hear or the sound we *make* to resonate in us.

Repetition

Another word for *meditation* in the Old Testament Hebrew is *siach*, or *suach*, which means "to rehearse, to repeat, to go over a matter in the mind," either silently or out loud. This word or concept appears frequently in a number of places, including Psalm 119. Verse 15 is an example: "I will meditate on Your precepts and regard Your ways." Verse 23 is another illustration: "Even though princes sit and talk against me, Your servant meditates on Your statutes." The psalmist declared to God that he would repeat the Lord's precepts and ways over and over again in his mind and heart.

So the second key concept in meditation is *repetition*, the practice of repeating a concept, a word or a verse to one's self until it takes on a life of its own, its meaning takes root in the heart and understanding springs forth as revelation at some deeper level. It is best to keep the concept, word or passage of Scripture brief and simple to maintain the simplicity and stillness of meditation in general. The use of many

HEARING GOD

words can engage the mind in details that lead away from the
simplicity of the Lord's presence and the still, small voice.
True Christian meditation is a way of causing the mind, the
heart, the subconscious and the human spirit to ponder the
things of God in order to unlock the depth of a given truth
until understanding comes at every level of one's being.

You can be programming software, driving nails, washing
dishes, changing diapers, doing homework or driving a car,
but you have fixed that concept, word or passage of Scripture in your mind at the start of the day and you repeat it to
yourself whenever you get the chance. As you do this, your
mind works on it, your spirit comprehends it and sooner or
later new information, fresh understanding and the word of
God begin to flow spontaneously.

The very structure of Hebrew poetry, the book of Psalms,
is built on repetition and is therefore carefully and intention-
ally designed for meditation. In English we rhyme words.
*Roses are red, violets are blue. The day is too short, the hours
too few*—bad poetry, but a good illustration! Hebrew rhymes
thoughts rather than words by juxtaposing two lines that
express the same basic concept in a creative way. Consider
Psalm 118:28, one of thousands of verses: "You are my God,
and I give thanks to You; You are my God, I extol You." This
verse expresses the idea of praising God in two artistically
contrasting ways. To "give thanks" and to "extol" are similar
ideas set alongside one another in a form of creative repetition that engages the heart in pondering and understanding
a truth in a deeper way.

Stillness

A number of passages point to *stillness*. Consider Psalm
4:4: "Tremble, and do not sin; meditate in your heart upon

your bed, and be still." So there comes a time to deliberately seek stillness in order to meditate. You must stop what you are doing, come away from the pervasive noise around you and begin to repeat a particular truth, desire or concept to yourself until it takes root and grows inside of you. Use sound such as meditative music, if necessary. The point is to come away from noise and activity. Stillness eliminates competing voices and noises and sets the stage for conversations with our Lord.

Close the door. Turn off the music—sometimes even the meditative music that can be helpful. Turn off the cell phone. Send the children outside. Tell your mind to be still. Empty yourself of all concerns, anxieties, purposes and plans that have filled your day and burdened your spirit. Set all these aside and open up to the Spirit of God. "The LORD preserves the simple; I was brought low, and He saved me. Return to your rest, O my soul, for the LORD has dealt bountifully with you" (Psalm 116:6–7). "My soul waits in silence for God only; from Him is my salvation" (Psalm 62:1). For some of us, meditation begins with instructing our inner selves to be still, and then in stillness we wait for the Lord.

Introduce a focus into your stillness. Jesus is before you. Jesus is in you. Touch that. Feel that. Own that. Let yourself "see" Him, figuratively speaking. To go back to an earlier point, let Jesus resonate within you as if He were a wonderful, vibrating and pulsing sound. He is there, having filled you with His Spirit. You need only become aware of Him. If you must repeat His name aloud or sing a song of simple praise in order to achieve stillness, do so, but above all, come into the quiet and wait for Him with no other agenda or goal than to rest in the Lord's presence.

Pondering

The final key word is *ponder.* Psalm 77:6 says, "I will re-member my song in the night; I will meditate with my heart, and my spirit ponders." To *ponder* is to "think deeply, to *feel,* to intuitively sense the truth and to let it resonate within you emotionally." In pondering you do not bully your mind for answers or strive to think things through, and you do not speak aloud concerning what you ponder. You simply allow an issue, a matter of God's Word, to roll around inside of you until it begins to make sense and until the revelation is released. In that sense, pondering relates closely to the practice of repetition. You may reason with your mind, but in pondering you seek to incorporate emotively into yourself the truth on which you have focused your attention.

I cannot begin, for instance, to explain intellectually the mystery of the Trinity—one God in three Persons—but in a pondering state I perceive it intuitively. It takes root in me, and I receive a depth of understanding from which I draw strength and faith for life and ministry. This is crucial to the prophetic voice because above all we must sense, feel and know the heart of the Lord who has entrusted us with His word.

A heart that ponders meanings deeply is a heart more open to hearing the voice of God. He speaks in many ways, but if our ability to ponder things is functionally sharp, then our intuitive capacity will be more alert to "hear." When the angel spoke to Mary to tell her of her destiny in bearing Jesus by a virginal conception, "she was very perplexed at this statement, and kept pondering what kind of salutation this was" (Luke 1:29). After the visit of the shepherds and their report of the angel choir that revealed the identity and destiny of her newborn son, "Mary treasured all these things, pondering them in her heart" (Luke 2:19). As one who pondered things in her heart, she qualified for the highest calling and the greatest prophetic act any human being would ever carry out.

Several years ago the Lord set me to pondering the cross and the blood of Jesus in this way. I have never been able to let it go. Day in and day out, it never leaves my mind as I ponder first the nature and character of Jesus and second, the meaning and impact of His death and resurrection. I do this because I want it all for me. I want everything the cross represents to become so much a part of me that I vibrate with it from the inside out. I want every aspect of my character to be captivated by it.

This, then, becomes the grid through which I learn to filter truth from falsehood, genuine God-breathed words from counterfeit. It keeps me simple, which has not been easy because I am a complicated man by nature. But simplicity in intimacy with God is the fountainhead of all that is truly prophetic. I therefore repeat the concepts of the cross and the blood in my mind, as well as passages like Galatians 2:20: "I have been crucified with Christ; and it is no longer I who live, but Christ lives in me; and the life which I now live in the flesh I live by faith in the Son of God, who loved me and gave Himself up for me." I let my spirit drink those words. I look—deeply—and then I look some more. I ponder until I ache. I focus on these things in almost the same way that I once obsessed over some beautiful girl when I was a teenager. I am consumed by them. In fact, I *choose* to be consumed by them.

I try to find stillness, quiet places in which to do this, but I also do it when driving my car, traveling on an airplane or walking from one place to another. I do it while I am writing a curriculum or working on a sermon. I do it even while watching a movie with my wife. I never let it go if I can possibly help it.

In pondering these truths, the revelation unfolds. Understanding flows at ever-deeper levels, and joy comes with it. Peace settles within me, and my character changes.

Yet I say with Paul,

> Brethren, I do not regard myself as having laid hold of it yet; but one thing I do: forgetting what lies behind and reaching forward to what lies ahead, I press on toward the goal for the prize of the upward call of God in Christ Jesus.
>
> Philippians 3:13–14

I wish I could say that I have become a great man of the Spirit. I am not, but I believe I have a reliable road map for reaching that goal.

The Choice

> I will extol You, my God, O King, and I will bless Your name forever and ever. Every day I will bless You, and I will praise Your name forever and ever. Great is the LORD, and highly to be praised, and His greatness is unsearchable. One generation shall praise Your works to another, and shall declare Your mighty acts. On the glorious splendor of Your majesty and on Your wonderful works, I will meditate.
>
> Psalm 145:1–5

What we say with our mouths repeatedly and rehearse in our minds reveals our true focus. These acts of repetition constitute evidence of what we have been meditating on, whether we knew we were meditating or not. We can repeat negativity until negativity becomes the atmosphere in which we live, the ether in which our emotions move. This affects our spiritual lives—what we believe about God, what we expect Him to do, how we worship, the intensity and purity of our love for our children, for our spouses, for one another and for the Lord.

But if we would learn to meditate—to resonate the sound, to repeat truth aloud and in our hearts, to be still before God, to ponder—on the wonderful things God has done, then the next verses of Psalm 145 become ours: "Men shall speak of the power of Your awesome acts, and I will tell of Your greatness. They shall eagerly utter the memory of Your abundant goodness and will shout joyfully of Your righteousness" (verses 6–7).

With meditation on the right things—the things of God—the prophetic word becomes a telling of the greatness of the Lord that encourages and engages others in the same joyous rehearsal of the truth.

8

NUMBERS 12

Visions and Dreams

In His rebuke to Aaron and Miriam for their arrogance in criticizing Moses, the Lord listed the means by which He communicates prophetically.

> He said, "Hear now My words: If there is a prophet among you, I, the LORD, shall make Myself known to him in a vision. I shall speak with him in a dream. Not so, with My servant Moses, He is faithful in all My household; with him I speak mouth to mouth, even openly, and not in dark sayings."
>
> Numbers 12:6–8

The ways in which God communicates prophetically, therefore, are visions, dreams, mouth to mouth (audible voice) and various forms of dark sayings.

Visions

Visions come in four main types. A vision can be any form of dramatic encounter with God, whether or not anything visual accompanies the encounter. It also can take the form of a mental image, a trance state or an open vision. It can even be comprised of a combination of any of these. As we examine each of these categories, try not to be too scientific or absolute about the definitions. God refuses to fit the boxes we try to pack Him into!

Visions as Encounters with God

The term *vision* seems to imply revelation by means of visual communication, but this is not always the case when Scripture uses the term. In many cases, the Bible reports only the words that flowed from the vision, with no mention of anything seen. Most often the message is straightforward and void of symbolism and requires little or no interpretation.

An example of this is Genesis 15:1–5:

> After these things the word of the LORD came to Abram in a vision, saying, "Do not fear, Abram, I am a shield to you; your reward shall be very great." Abram said, "O Lord GOD, what will You give me, since I am childless, and the heir of my house is Eliezer of Damascus?" And Abram said, "Since You have given no offspring to me, one born in my house is my heir." Then behold, the word of the LORD came to him, saying, "This man will not be your heir; but one who will come forth from your own body, he shall be your heir." And He took him outside and said, "Now look toward the heavens, and count the stars, if you are able to count them." And He said to him, "So shall your descendants be."

What did Abram see? Did he see anything at all? Scripture does not say.

Similarly Samuel received his calling as a prophet in an encounter reported in Scripture as a vision, although words alone are recorded. Here we find no symbolism and virtually nothing to interpret:

> The LORD said to Samuel, "Behold, I am about to do a thing in Israel at which both ears of everyone who hears it will tingle. In that day I will carry out against Eli all that I have spoken concerning his house, from beginning to end. For I have told him that I am about to judge his house forever for the iniquity which he knew, because his sons brought a curse on themselves and he did not rebuke them. Therefore I have sworn to the house of Eli that the iniquity of Eli's house shall not be atoned for by sacrifice or offering forever." So Samuel lay down until morning. Then he opened the doors of the house of the LORD. But Samuel was afraid to tell the vision to Eli.
>
> 1 Samuel 3:11–15

In both of these instances, although nothing visual was reported, it seems clear that the Lord did appear in some measurable way. In the absence of anything we would call a vision, Scripture nevertheless uses the term *vision* to describe what happened. The word *vision* is therefore not limited to what can be seen. It can in fact be used to describe any tangible encounter with God that includes elements external to the one who receives it and in which God communicates in a clear and unmistakable manner.

Mental Images, Trance States and Open Visions

Visions can take three other forms. We can receive internal *mental images* on the screens of our minds, we can be caught up in *trance states* in which it is even possible to be transported out of the body or we can experience *open visions* from God that we see externally like a movie on a screen. The line dividing these three kinds of vision is often blurred, and it accomplishes little to categorize them when that blurring is present. It matters only that the Lord communicates and that His servant hears.

Experience has shown me that the more internal the vision, the more symbolic it will likely be, although that rule does not always hold. A vision heavy with symbolism must be interpreted, but there are at least as many visions with literal meaning in Scripture as there are visions in need of interpretation.

Because there is so much opportunity for the human imagination to become involved—something to which prophetic people are especially vulnerable—mental images are the least reliable of these three forms of revelatory vision. Mental imagery presents too much opportunity for our sins, judgments, hopes, dreams and fleshly imaginations to color the picture. The character and wholeness of the recipient therefore become crucial to the purity of any revelation received in this way. Further, I see scant scriptural precedent for merely mental revelatory visions, but God can and does speak in any manner He wishes. Such visions, for all their uncertainty, can therefore be powerful and useful.

On Sunday, April 23, 2006, worship at our church had moved into a time of an intense sense of the presence of God. In a mental image, I saw a man's chest with a slot in it, like the slot on our computers or musical synthesizers into which we put CD-ROMs to upgrade or install software. I saw a hand insert a CD into the slot. I asked the Lord what it meant, if anything, and I "heard" Him say He wanted to give a download of new faith to those who needed it—that it was a time to trust Him anew in a season of blessing. I described to the congregation what I had seen and invited any who needed that download of faith to come forward—all in the context of the continuing flow of worship. I was amazed to see two-thirds of the congregation come streaming forward. Filled to overflowing with the Spirit, my son, our youth pastor, took the microphone and led us in a powerful time of prayer, impartation and healing as the ministry team moved through the crowd praying for people.

All this was sparked by a vision received as a mental image. Notice that as a mental image the message came couched in symbolism that rendered the vision useless until interpreted. It is not within the scope of this book to teach extensively on the meaning of various symbols and how to interpret them. Obviously a study of scriptural symbolism would be useful, but for the most part, interpretation of visions and dreams (to be discussed later) is not a science with consistently predictable results. Rather, it is a prophetic gift of the Spirit. For this reason, when I received the vision I immediately asked the Lord what it meant. The fruit that flowed from it proved the accuracy of both the vision and its interpretation.

Trance states are obviously much more infrequent than mere mental images. With a mental image, the recipient retains both consciousness and control. In a trance state, the recipient finds himself or herself controlled by the Holy Spirit and somewhat, if not totally, removed from awareness of the physical world. The apostle Paul spoke of such an experience in 2 Corinthians 12:2–4:

> I know a man in Christ who fourteen years ago—whether in the body I do not know, or out of the body I do not know, God knows—such a man was caught up to the third heaven. And I know how such a man—whether in the body or apart from the body I do not know, God knows—was caught up into Paradise and heard inexpressible words, which a man is not permitted to speak.

I do not believe Paul meant the man was transported to the third heaven physically. In a trance state, it is possible to be taken out of the body. The Lord does not permit us to seek this kind of thing on our own, but if He Himself initiates it in order to deliver a revelation, we can embrace the experience.

In Revelation 1:10, John the apostle wrote, "I was in the Spirit on the Lord's day, and I heard behind me a loud voice like the sound of a trumpet." I have no doubt that this particular reference to "in the Spirit" implies a God-inspired trance state. Visions of heaven and the end times resulted, all communicated in mysterious symbolism that has inspired intense debate from that time until now.

Although I have never experienced a true trance state, I know people who have. In renewal meetings it is not uncommon to see someone overcome by God and rendered senseless to the physical world for an extended period of time. In reality he or she has been caught up in a life-changing visionary encounter with God. A story common to many is that God showed them their broken past in relation to a father or mother and then healed them of the pain by means of a vision of themselves in Jesus' or the Father's arms. All this occurs in the context of what can only be described as a trance state. A wonderfully enriched relationship with God results.

Daniel 5 includes an example of an open vision. Belshazzar, king of Babylon, hosted a banquet at which he brought out the holy utensils from the destroyed Temple in Jerusalem so his people could drink from them in honor of "the gods of gold and silver, of bronze, iron, wood and stone" (verse 4). In verse 5 comes the open vision: "Suddenly the fingers of a man's hand emerged and began writing opposite the lampstand on the plaster of the wall of the king's palace, and the king saw the back of the hand that did the writing." Because no one understood the language in which the writing appeared, the king summoned Daniel to interpret the vision. The message in the vision declared the impending destruction of Belshazzar's kingdom.

In 2005 I underwent a surgery to remove six inches of my colon. As I recovered at home, the pain subsided in all but one of the several incisions. So intense was the pain that I began to worry that something might be wrong. As I lay in bed one afternoon in a state of semiconsciousness, a warrior appeared beside me dressed in armor reminiscent of a Star Wars stormtrooper, but in bright multicolors rather than the white they wore in the movies. He climbed onto my bed and straddled me on his knees, reached down to the location of the painful incision and seized a knife embedded there. Pain like I had never known shot through me, and I sat straight up in bed gasping for breath.

At first I took this open vision to be a demonic attack and began to pray accordingly, but after an hour or so I had settled down enough to realize that the pain had vanished. It never returned. I believe this incident fell somewhere between an open vision and a dream state and that an angel of the Lord came to effect my healing. The revelation component of the vision had to do with understanding how much God loved me. Nothing in my ministry had been going well at the time, and at an emotional level I had begun to question the quality of His love. Visions are not therefore solely a means of revelation, but can be vehicles for healing, as well. They can have a physical effect.

While he was still Saul, the terror of all believers, the apostle Paul received an open vision of Jesus on the Damascus road in which the Lord revealed to him the truth about Himself (see Acts 9). Blinded by the encounter, Paul remained unable to see for three days before Ananias came to pray for him. This open vision and its aftermath set the course of Paul's life, and he became the greatest of all the apostles—the most significant crafter and interpreter of our faith. An open vision brought life-changing revelation accompanied by a measurable physical consequence.

Note once again that the more a vision leans toward the "open" category, as opposed to mere mental image, the less symbolism is present and the less it needs interpretation. And open visions can have physical consequences for those who receive them.

Dreams

We believers rightly regard dreams as a means of receiving revelation from God. Unfortunately, this has led to an imbalance in the weight and credit we give to dreaming. In some quarters of the prophetic movement we have become obsessed with dreams and their interpretation at the expense of true intimacy with God. Dreams have become a thing in themselves.

In reality, *some* dreams are God-inspired while *most* dreams serve other purposes necessary to mental and emotional health. Discerning the difference can be difficult. I hope the following explanations help to make it easier.

Natural Dreams

Not all dreams are God-inspired! Most are *natural dreams*.

As expressions of our own flesh, dreams can often be infected with our sin in ways that lie to us if we make the mistake of assuming they all come from God. When Jeremiah, for example, prophesied destruction upon Israel in judgment for their sin, those who thought themselves prophetic dreamed fleshly dreams reflective of their own desires to avoid disaster.

"But as for you, do not listen to your prophets, your diviners, your dreamers, your soothsayers or your sorcerers who speak to you, saying, 'You will not serve the king of Babylon.' For they prophesy a lie to you in order to remove you far from your land; and I will drive you out and you will perish."

Jeremiah 27:9–10

In an article published in *Reader's Digest* in February 2006, author Michael J. Weiss reported a number of conclusions drawn by current dream researchers. Weiss said that dreams are a means for the subconscious mind to communicate with the conscious mind. These two levels of consciousness work together to help us learn, remember and solve problems. For instance, dreaming can be a means of internally rehearsing for a crisis or stressful event the conscious mind knows is coming. Weiss quoted Rosalind Cartwright, Ph.D., chairman of the psychology department at Rush University Medical Center in Chicago, who said that dreams are part of our "mood regulatory system." Dreams help us work through the emotional situations we find ourselves facing on a day-to-day basis. She said, "It's like having a built-in therapist."

According to Weiss, current researchers have concluded that dream symbolism is by no means universal but is in fact unique to the individual. Remember this for later discussion! Weiss cited research showing that even the colors seen in dreams reflect not a universal symbolism but rather the emotional state of the dreamer at the time.

My own observations lead me to conclude that our brains are like complex organic computers. As we move through our waking lives, they accumulate bits and pieces of excess information, unresolved anxieties, emotions, thoughts, melodies and more. In our dreams the subconscious mind gathers these things together, organizes them into story packages and processes them, thus cleaning the computer and preparing it for another day.

A related function of dreams is to alert us to unresolved issues lodged deep in the heart. One young adult told me of the bloody and terrifying nightmares he was having and that these were the only dreams he ever dreamed. This had been going on for years. As I listened, I knew that his subconscious mind was alerting him to the urgency of dealing with the terror and destruction rooted in his hideous and abusive childhood. We had been working with him for a long time to get him into our counseling department. His dreams focused the urgency of it.

These primary functions of dreaming explain why insanity develops when something prevents us from dreaming so that the release dreaming provides is blocked. Therefore, I reiterate that not all dreams are God dreams. If the content of a dream too directly reflects an experience, a fear, a hope, a struggle or a desire of my own without a clear direction included or some element that clearly does not arise from my own experience or emotional state, then I regard it as a message from my own inner man alerting me to a need. It is a natural dream.

I often dream, for instance, that I have enrolled in college and that the end of the semester has come. I am doing well in all my classes, but final exams are upon me and I suddenly discover that I have completely forgotten one of my classes. In fact, I have never even attended it. Now it is too late to catch up, and I know I am going to fail. The awful feeling can linger for half a day after I wake up. This is nothing more than an anxiety dream, not a message from God. It expresses my inner fears when I am under pressure. A similar recurring anxiety dream portrays me standing before a group of people to preach when I suddenly realize I have forgotten to

put on my pants. In the dream I am always terribly embar-
rassed, but I cannot figure out how to leave the stage. This
is no message from God warning me to remember to get
dressed before preaching, but rather it is my subconscious
mind processing my performance anxieties.

Direct Dreams

While realizing that most dreams are natural dreams, I
actually do give great weight to dreams as a means of revelation from God. Scripture contains two kinds of revelatory dreams. The first is direct and unadorned in its lack of
symbolism. *Direct dreams* require no interpretation. The
angel appears to Joseph in a dream in Matthew 1 to command him clearly and without symbolism to take Mary as
his wife after she has become pregnant with Jesus. Again
in a dream, the angel orders him to go to Egypt to escape
Herod's campaign of murder. The instructions delivered in
these dreams bear no possibility of any interpretation other
than the clear meaning of the words. This kind of dream
seems to be rare, and I can honestly say that I have never
dreamed in this way.

Symbolic Dreams

In Scripture, dreams given to believers tend to be direct, as
is evidenced by Joseph's two dreams noted above. *Symbolic
dreams* needing prophetic interpretation, on the other hand,
are most often given to unbelievers—although this is not an
absolute. The dreams given to Pharaoh and Belshazzar are
examples of symbolic dreams given to unbelievers.

Obviously, this raises troubling questions as to the dominant character of the dreams most believers receive today. As
a result, I ask myself how dysfunctional—or even alienated

from God—we have become if the majority of our dreams from Him must be presented in symbolism.

According to the scriptural record, dream interpretation is a prophetic gift rather than a learned skill or science. In Scripture, when someone dreams such a dream, a prophet must be called upon to interpret its meaning. The gift of interpretation can be trained, and skill can be added to it, but no amount of knowledge can substitute for it.

Pharaoh's diviners and wise men, for instance, were given the same dream and had roughly equal knowledge of dream symbols, yet they failed to interpret a dream that Joseph found easily transparent (see Genesis 41). Joseph explained the operation of his gift: "It is not in me; God will give Pharaoh a favorable answer" (Genesis 41:16). The difference between Joseph and Pharaoh's wise men lay not in their knowledge of the science of interpretation, but in the prophetic gift from God.

Divinely inspired symbolic dreams can include dramatic encounters with God, including audible voices (not "dream sound"), even when the message is couched in symbolism. Audible voices in a dream indicate the presence of an angelic messenger.

In 2004 I dreamed I was in a restaurant eating dinner with my wife when a large man approached our table and announced loudly in an audible voice, "I am a member of Mike's board. Mike has died, and we want you to come and pastor the church." ("Mike" is not the name the angel actually spoke; the name he gave was the pastor of a church that had once been a center for revival in our city.) The announcement of his death reflected the fact that Mike had withdrawn his former support of renewal and of the movement of the Spirit and now stood in opposition. The angel was calling me to assume at least a portion of the office and mission that Mike had laid down. This dream illustrates a mixture of dramatic encounter with symbolic language requiring interpretation.

In July 2005 I dreamed that a doctor informed me, "You don't even know who's coming from the right side because you can't hear." He told me I needed a hearing aid for my right ear. I protested that I could hear music just fine but admitted that under normal circumstances I did not hear as well on that side. The doctor responded, "Then don't wear it when doing music, but wear it at other times and you'll hear more." In some cases the right side represents the ministry side, the side for the exercise of authority. As a worship leader, songwriter and musician I was hearing God just fine. The dream indicated God's desire to expand the prophetic aspect of my ministry in hearing Him and that His authority in that portion of my calling would increase. In the months that followed, God did, in fact, expand the prophetic side of my ministry into areas of insight and levels of accuracy I had never known.

Dream Interpretation

Although dream symbols are neither absolute nor universal in their meaning, some symbols can mean the same thing most of the time. Although this is not the place for an extended dissertation on dream symbolism, a few pointers are in order.

It is always wise to begin with biblical images and biblical numbers. Seven, for instance, represents fullness or perfection. Forty is a number for wilderness. Three stands for the Trinity, the Godhead. Rivers and wind can indicate the flow of the Spirit of God. Fire can symbolize cleansing or judgment. Gold stands for purity, while silver speaks of redemption.

In spite of researchers' denials of the existence of universal symbols, many extrabiblical symbols do have fairly common meanings. A house can often stand for the household of one's life, especially when the house is a current residence or a childhood home. A basement might point to hidden issues.

Prior to experiencing a significant inner healing, I once dreamed that I lived in a wonderful home with just one flaw in the basement. I could not repair the flaw because the only way to get to it was through a locked door on the outside of the house to which I had no key. An angel wearing a repairman's uniform came with a key, opened it and went inside. Another angel explained to me that the first angel had come to make the repair. Weeks later I experienced a dramatic healing of a childhood issue that changed my life.

Automobiles frequently represent ministries. Buses can indicate large ministries affecting numbers of people. Trains can stand for movements involving collections of allied ministries all going in the same direction. Spiders can indicate witchcraft. Cats can represent independent thinking or willfulness. Blue can symbolize revelation. Red can stand for anger, wisdom or power. These are just a few examples out of a great many common symbols. For those who wish to study dream symbolism and interpretation further, I believe that Streams Ministries (John Paul Jackson) offers the best and most effective training programs and informational materials.

Finally, when interpreting dreams it helps to understand the outline of a person's life. Symbols may reflect real-life situations and experiences and can therefore be as unique to the individual as researchers claim. I am a musician, for instance, so for me, microphones and sound systems represent communication—how I am heard or not heard. For a person who works in a burger joint, a hamburger could symbolize something at which he or she labored in life. For someone in a different situation, a hamburger could represent spiritual food being offered or consumed. Symbols do vary in meaning from individual to individual according to life experience.

Basic dream interpretation, therefore, involves four components. First, gain a working understanding of biblical symbolism. Second, expand your knowledge of common extrabiblical symbols, some of which can be reasoned out based on the function inherent in the symbol (i.e., automobile = taking people somewhere = ministry). Third, identify with the person whose dream it is. Feel with him or her and then objectively explore the shape of his or her life. Fourth and most important, ask God what it all means and how it all fits together, and then listen for the revelation.

9

THE VOICE OF GOD

God speaks to individual prophets in uniquely different ways. No single formula for hearing Him works for every person. With Moses communication went *mouth to mouth*—an open form of communication. Others received the word through various forms of *dark speech*—a category of concealment demanding revelation. Dreams and visions also entered the mix, as we have already discussed.

Mouth to Mouth

In Numbers 12 the Lord clearly differentiates between the way He communicates with ordinary prophets and the way He communicated with Moses. God gives dreams and visions to the ordinary prophet while reserving mouth-to-mouth communication for those with the qualifications God recognized in Moses.

As opposed to mental voices or impressions, mouth-to-mouth communication indicates audible speech heard in the natural. God spoke to Moses in an audible voice at the burning bush—no symbolism and nothing incorporeal. The bush, the flames and the voice were real. The whole experience manifested in the natural world. Similarly, the apostle Paul heard the audible voice of Jesus while lying helpless in the dirt on the Damascus road. Because it manifested in the objective world, those traveling with him heard the sound, although the message was for Paul alone: "The men who traveled with him stood speechless, hearing the voice but seeing no one" (Acts 9:7).

Abraham received direct, mouth-to-mouth communication from God, and Scripture says of him in James 2:23, "'Abraham believed God, and it was reckoned to him as righteousness,' and he was called the friend of God." How many of us actually have entered such a state of trustworthiness before God that we have become not just His children and not merely His servants, but friends in whom He can confide? Could this be one reason that men of God in Scripture experienced mostly direct dreams while believers today receive mainly the kind of symbolic dreams common to unbelievers in the scriptural record? We have missed something Moses and the other great biblical prophets understood.

On the basis of these biblical accounts, I believe the audible voice is mostly—but not necessarily exclusively—reserved for high calling and, in most cases, high calling coupled with faithfulness like that of Moses: "He is faithful in all My household" (Numbers 12:7). Or perhaps it would be more accurate to say that God reserves high calling for those who are faithful like Moses and that the audible voice therefore comes to those who are faithful in the way of Moses. Paul, on the other hand, heard the audible voice of God before he could have been deemed faithful in all the Lord's household, but it came in the context of a dramatic divine intervention to turn his life from destruction to useful service in a high calling.

What God described to Aaron and Miriam in Numbers 12 implies not just occasional but ongoing audible communication with Moses. For this, the key requirement is certainly radical faithfulness. God insinuated in less than subtle terms that Aaron and Miriam had better remember their unfaithful participation in the making of the golden calf while Moses was away on the mountain with God, receiving the Law. It was as if He said to them, "Moses is faithful in all My household, but you committed the ultimate compromise not so long ago!" Demonstrated inconsistency versus proven faithfulness constituted the difference between how Aaron and Miriam heard from God and how Moses received the Word.

Depending on the situation, therefore, there are three keys to audible communication with God. First, mouth-to-mouth communication can take the form of a dramatic intervention to set the course of a life that has been chosen for a strong destiny. Second, in most reported cases in Scripture where God speaks audibly to a person, high calling is involved. Moses played the key role in crafting the faith of the entire nation of Israel even to this day. He led a group of slaves out of Egypt and molded them into a people capable of taking the Promised Land. Paul became the greatest of all the apostles. His impact on all that we call "Christian" towers over that of any other apostle. I do not believe high calling is an absolute requirement for hearing the audible voice, but I do believe the audible voice is a requirement for certain kinds of high calling. Third, the person to whom God communicates mouth to mouth in an ongoing way must exhibit stable and established faithfulness.

Outside of these three keys, I do not necessarily rule out the audible voice of God, but in the absence of all these three keys, I strongly suspect schizophrenia, delusion or demonic influence. Diligent testing is required.

Dark Sayings

God speaks to prophets in one other way: the mysterious category Scripture calls "dark sayings." This phrase describes communication that is in some way concealed, or "darkened," so that meaning and content must be sought out and pondered. God masks the message so that we must seek Him more deeply in order to understand. He did not need to speak this way with Moses because Moses was already deeply intimate with Him. With Moses He could speak directly. But for most of us, "darkening" is something like a divine trick God plays to inspire us to press closer as we seek understanding.

And it works! In the spring of 2006, for instance, I woke up one morning with a sense of impending doom that I did not understand. As I began to pray I realized it did not feel personal, and so I asked the Lord what it was. Because God is still working with me to turn my density into destiny, the answer was not immediately forthcoming. I am a tough nut to crack sometimes, so I spent some considerable time in prayer, quieting myself, meditating on the Lord and seeking that state of rest in which the still, small voice can be heard. Finally, in my mind I heard (not audibly, as I am no Moses), "High temperatures will reach critical levels this year. In many places fires will devour. Winds will fan the flames."

As is my custom, in the evening I checked the CNN website for the daily news. One of the headlines announced that critically high temperatures and high winds were driving wildfires in southern Oklahoma and that officials had lost count of the number of homes that had been lost. The following week, as a result of the same conditions, in excess of one million acres of Texas real estate went up in smoke. A dark saying in the form of an intuitive sense of something I did not understand led to revelation for the purpose of prayer, but first I had to seek the Lord for the meaning of what I sensed. The act of seeking worked to build my relationship with Him in intimacy, which is what God wanted all along.

Dark sayings in the form of intuitive sensing can create difficulties. They come to us through our capacity to burden bear and thus affect our moods—and as I have said, we prophetic types can be a moody lot! Self-focus must be substantially conquered in the prophetic person so that emotional self-absorption does not lead him or her to interpret this kind of sensing as a personal mood by which to be trapped and consumed. In the example above, I could have been devoured by personal fear and thereby completely missed the point. More importantly, emotional self-absorption would have hindered my ministry to others later in the day. We must learn to sort the external from the internal, something many of us have yet to master. This is true especially when the intuitive sense hangs on for an extended period of time without a clear explanation from God.

When I was a teenager, I traveled as a musician with a rock group. Often in the wee hours of the morning as we drove home from some distant "gig," I would fall asleep at the wheel, and my foot would push the accelerator pedal to the floor. Again and again when this happened I would hear my father's voice call loudly, "Loren!" His voice would startle me awake just in time to avoid running my car under the tail end of a semitrailer or some other vehicle. The next day my father would tell me, "The Lord woke me up at about three this morning with a sense of danger and told me to pray for you," and I knew that 3:00 A.M. was the exact time I had heard his voice. He received only a sense of danger, a dark saying, that prompted him to seek an answer from the Lord. More than once it saved my life.

Senses like these are nudges—some of them urgent—to pick up the phone, so to speak. God is calling! A dark saying is only part of the message—not enough to go on, but enough to drive us to seek connection with the One who summons us in order to receive the fullness.

The immature tend to think that every feeling they experience is the voice of God. Inconsistency results. One woman who pops in and out of our church and thinks herself a prophetess provides a good example. "God told me that this is my church, and I've been assigned to you as a prophetess." Less than a month passes before God has told her to move on to another church. But I know that she will be back before much time has passed and that she will have the same or a similar word. It is never the voice of God; it is her own feelings that she deifies, not knowing the difference. Whenever she finds that the position for which she hungers is not available to her, then "God" tells her to move on.

Because of the dangers, God has established and prescribed a course of training and relationship for discipline to which prophetic people must submit for their own safety and for that of the Body of Christ. We will examine this more later. Meanwhile, as we discussed in chapter 2 when talking about using the Lord's name in vain, it is wiser and safer to say, "I think the Lord may be saying . . ." and then submit to the checks and balances the Lord has ordained to test us.

Mental visions, which we discussed earlier in this chapter, are a form of dark sayings. The picture of a man with a slot in his chest and the hand of God inserting a CD-ROM had to be pondered and its meaning sought out. The quest for the meaning of the mystery drew me closer to God.

Symbolic dreams are a form of dark saying. They come to us with masked meaning, which prompts us to seek the presence of God for the interpretation.

The "Nathan Prophet"

Normally, one ought to put in print only those things he or she understands well. In this section, I violate that principle. I do not fully understand what you are about to read, but for the sake of those who would pursue it, I must at least point us in a direction.

In 1988 Bob Jones visited the church I pastored in Idaho. At some point during the conference that week he made a strange statement to me: "I have my little dreams and visions, but you're a Nathan prophet. You just know things." It stayed with me, and I have pondered it ever since. "Nathan prophet" is Bob's phrase, based on the way in which Nathan appeared to "just know" the sin of David with Bathsheba and the murder of Uriah, her husband. Here is what I tentatively understand concerning what Bob calls the "Nathan prophet."

Many times over the years, I have just "known" things, as Bob would put it. In the years prior to AD 2000, for instance, while many prophetic voices declared an impending Y2K computer disaster, I just "knew" it would never happen, and in knowing it, I stood against the prevailing prophetic stream. Later I confirmed my knowing by researching how computers actually work, but initially it was this mysterious knowing. Please do not mistake this as a statement of pride. Many of those who advocated storing up food and supplies in order to prepare to minister to victims of the disaster have borne a great deal more fruit in the Kingdom of God than I have! I am humbled before them and cite this only as an example of a "Nathan" kind of knowing.

Prior to the 2004 presidential election I knew with settled certainty, without words, dreams or visions, that President Bush would be reelected, but with difficulty, and that his second term would not be like his first, that it would be fraught with difficulties beyond the ability of any human being to fully understand or solve. History has unfolded in just this way.

Another example concerns the war in Iraq. I am not qualified to pass judgment on the rightness or wrongness of that war, and I do not intend the following statement to be taken as that kind of judgment. I know only that in my spirit I had a foreboding during the buildup to the invasion that went beyond a normal apprehension of the hideous nature of war. I knew that it would inflame the Arab world in hatred and that it would cost the United States in ways we could not calculate. Today hatred against the United States in the Muslim world has escalated. Our nation itself has been deeply divided. We have paid a high price. This kind of "knowing" calls us to prayer for the mitigation or redemption of the destructive consequences the prophet sees coming.

On a more individual level, twenty years ago I spoke with a mother concerned for her son. He appeared troubled, and his life seemed to be headed for a serious train wreck. By contrast, her daughter behaved well, obeyed her parents and displayed a sweet disposition. Yet one day I found myself saying to this mother, "Bob will be fine. Don't worry about him. It's Mary who will give you the trouble." Twelve years later she told me I had been absolutely right. Bob had turned his life around and was serving the Lord, while Mary chose

THE VOICE OF GOD

to lose herself in every kind of sin a parent fears. Fortunately she, too, finally began to turn back to the Lord after a long sojourn on the dark side, in large part due to the prayers of her mother. My point is that in the prophetic moment, without feelings, words or visions, I just knew what was to come.

I understand little concerning this kind of knowing. What I do know is confined to two categories. First, I believe it is possible in our union with Jesus to be so deeply of one heart and one Spirit with Him that what He knows, we know—not in intellectual terms and certainly not in omniscience but at the level of righteousness. This knowing discerns right from wrong, gives insight into trends and events and reveals certain things to come. Paul wrote, "For who has known the mind of the Lord, that he will instruct Him? But we have the mind of Christ" (1 Corinthians 2:16). I suspect this verse has something to do with the kind of prophetic knowing I am describing here. Perhaps another paradigm might be the depth of relationship I share with my wife. Our oneness enables us to sense one another's thoughts and feelings, even at a distance. Should it not be so with our Lord?

The second category has to do with all that the Lord deposits in us over a lifetime. He gives us His Spirit and shapes our character. He teaches us His Word. We understand the truth of it intellectually, but it also works to conform us to the image of Jesus if we choose to receive it properly. It tunes our thoughts to His frequency, so to speak. This process of deposit and shaping affects our emotional makeup, character, personality and intellect. The more these elements of our human nature conform to Him, the more easily He can speak into us via all the deposits He has made. His revelation may not come to us in words, dreams or visions. We simply know what we know, and we call it "hearing from God."

Some would say this "knowing" is what we often think of as "the witness of the Spirit," or a word of knowledge. I have experienced those, too, and I can tell you that prophetic knowing is more than that. There is a difference.

Does the inanimate sword receive and understand intelligible direction from the swordsman who wields it? Or does it respond to the hand of the warrior for the simple reason that it was designed to do so? By contrast, the trouble with a living human sword is that it has a will of its own—the capacity to reason and feel and have a relationship with the Master. This will has been steeped in sin and rebellion from conception so that, contrary to its design, it cooperates with the Master only with difficulty. Should not redemption lead us to that place of willing submission in which we simply "know" the will of the Master and respond with easy grace?

Journaling

I keep a prayer and listening journal in which I write down everything that comes to me in all the forms of communication I have outlined above. In my journal I add one more form of hearing that does not necessarily fit any of the other categories: I listen for Scripture references. I am mnemonically challenged when it comes to remembering addresses, so I usually forget the content of any given reference until I look it up. In most cases the particular reference I feel impressed to look up speaks directly to something that has been on my heart, or it describes something for which I need to be watching. Occasionally it reiterates and affirms a promise the Lord has made.

In 1971 I had been arguing with the Lord concerning my calling. I never wanted to be a pastor. As a preacher's kid I had seen the Church from the dirty underside, and I did not want to go there. But through a complicated set of circumstances, the Lord had limited my options so that after much struggle I finally asked Him directly, "Lord, do You want me to be a pastor?" I "heard" mentally, "Hebrews 5:6." When I looked it up it read, "You are a priest forever according to the order of Melchizedek." I was smart enough to know that in its context this verse speaks of Jesus, but I could hardly miss the point for me personally. I finished my bachelor's degree in music, married the girl who had known from childhood that she would be a pastor's wife and enrolled at Fuller Theological Seminary.

In one instance (among many) in 2006 God impressed me to look up Psalm 59:1–4:

> Deliver me from my enemies, O my God; set me securely on high away from those who rise up against me. Deliver me from those who do iniquity and save me from men of bloodshed. For behold, they have set an ambush for my life; fierce men launch an attack against me, not for my transgression nor for my sin, O LORD, for no guilt of mine, they run and set themselves against me. Arouse Yourself to help me, and see!

I knew from long experience to begin praying concerning an attack to come in the form of unjustified accusation. Within days a precious member of our church began projecting unresolved issues with his father onto me when I failed to relate to him according to some specific and unreasonable expectations he held. Because I had been warned beforehand to pray, he came to me just two days later filled with humble apologies for being wrongly upset with me. We embraced, and the incident ended on solid ground.

I record in my journal, therefore, all the Scriptures I am impressed to look up. Over time I may see that they form a pattern of something the Lord is trying to show me. Warnings and promises unfold. Often He sends comfort in the form of just the right passage for the moment.

I also write down the things I hear the Lord saying to me mentally, such as the word concerning the fires and the wind. Once I am in that quiet place, I listen and try to honor the first things that come into my mind like whispers on a breeze. Sometimes it seems as though I must reach out quickly to catch them before they get lost in the background noise of my mind. Most often this forms a conversation with God. I speak and He responds, or He speaks and then I respond. I also write down my dreams and their possible interpretations.

The first reason I do all this is so that I do not forget what God has been saying to me. I find it too easy as time passes to alter memories of words I have received in order to fit what I want to hear. I want to avoid what I call "rubber prophecies"—the ones we stretch or reinterpret to fit circumstances as they develop so we can fool ourselves into thinking we were right when we were not.

My brother Mark and I, for example, once had a conversation about my former church in Idaho and its long lingering death after I left. I had "heard" from God that this church would grow and thrive and have a world impact. Mark suggested that perhaps the reason it never happened was that the people refused to make the choices that would have made that possible. I told him that, yes, the people refused to make the necessary choices to grow into wholeness and maturity. But I also told him that I would not stretch or alter those prophecies to make them fit the circumstances. If they had been true words from God, then they would have come to pass. I knew it would be wrong to lessen the impact of the failure of those words by stretching them to fit the reality.

I had to face the fact that I had "heard" not from God but through the filter of my own ambitions.

I therefore write down what I receive so I can remember exactly what I heard and render myself less susceptible to stretching things. Self-deception leading to delusions of grandeur is one of the most common quicksand piles into which prophetic people fall. Been there! Done that!

The second reason I journal is that it provides a means of training my senses to discern true from false. Hebrews 5:14 says, "But solid food is for the mature, who because of practice have their senses trained to discern good and evil." As illustrated in my conversation with my brother, I can review things in my journals that I believe the Lord has spoken and compare those things to the ways in which reality actually unfolds. In most cases where I have been proven wrong, I can note the "taste" the word had when I received it and train my senses accordingly. The word felt mostly right at the time but underneath was a taint, almost like the "undertaste" in some artificially flavored foods. If I can train myself to identify and remember that taste, then I can identify it again.

Over the years I have been in many meetings in which things spoken under supposed prophetic anointing seemed right, but I detected that undertaste in my spirit. Even now there are times when I think I might be hearing from God, but the faint sense of taint is present and I must force myself to pay attention to it. Through practice, we can learn to separate true from false by training our senses to detect the taint. Journaling helps.

Be warned! Journaling can be brutally embarrassing. I have a whole shelf of journals from my messy twenties and thirties that inform me in stark black-and-white terms that on a distressing number of occasions I "heard" exactly what

I wanted to hear. In those journals it becomes clear, for instance, that God wanted me to move away from northern Idaho, but I did not want to hear it. I therefore "heard" the promises of growth and prosperity for my ministry there that I have referred to above. I heard these things even while the ministry withered around me. I had a lot of dying to do, and even more learning to trust the Lord. I heard a lot of things accurately, as well, but I was much more accurate in areas that did not matter so much to me personally.

The third reason I journal is that it keeps me from being dominated by the emotions of the moment. Too many of us bounce from one direction for life and ministry to another with little stability because we have built nothing into our lives and practices to remind us of what God has said concerning us over the long run. Consequently, momentary feelings dominate us and our fruit suffers. The problem is that feelings by themselves are inconsistent and often chemically induced. In looking back over my journals, I am reminded of the consistent direction the Lord has set for my life and how that has never changed, no matter how my own feelings varied.

I also journal the prophetic words spoken over me by others. Again, this serves as a benchmark against which to sort true from false. For the most part, words spoken over me have been consistent in their content, mapping out a destiny that has yet to unfold in real substance. I see signs of fulfillment, but not yet the fullness. Nevertheless, the consistency of what has been said demands respect and consideration, and so I pray and prepare.

Finally, journaling helps me focus my attention. As a pastor, worship leader, musician, community figure, mentor, author, husband, father and grandfather, my life is filled with more demands than I can juggle all at once. When I sit down to pray, all these things rush to the forefront, clamoring for my attention. Journaling puts something concrete in front of me in the form of paper or computer screen, while the act of writing serves to hold all that intruding noise at bay so I can focus on just one thing—intimacy with God. It is a discipline, and discipline is the way of life. For the prophetic person, discipline can be his or her salvation.

Conclusion

All the things I have mentioned in this chapter form a kind of self-checking mosaic that works together with input from trusted friends in the faith to contribute to a cleaner perception of the voice of God. I often hear phrases or paragraphs in a conversational way and I write them down. When I have written them down, I will receive a prompting to look up a particular verse that confirms what I have heard. A dream will drive me to seek the Lord more deeply for understanding of its meaning. Subsequent events will reveal the interpretation, or God will reveal the interpretation in my times of prayer through direct words or verses to look up. Sometimes the word simply dawns on me as revelation. Occasionally a friend provides the insight. What I believe I have heard must be checked against the discernment of others with whom I have relationship—and not those who flatter me but those with the courage and security to challenge me! No modern-day prophetic person can afford to operate in isolation. Delusion will certainly result. All the tests outlined earlier in this book must be applied.

Hearing God is not a science or a method but rather a function of relationship. In that sense, hearing from God is a fluid dance of elements that move together in different ways to connect us with Him at every level of our being.

God is a person, not an object or an impersonal force. If I were to relate to my wife by means of some kind of artificial methodology or set of absolutes meant to interpret the signals she sends me at the many levels of our union, she would feel as if the relationship had been damaged and would say something like, "What's the matter with you? Will you get real?" I would have missed her as a person. Distance rather than intimacy would result. The same is true of our relationship with God.

That being understood, I will close this chapter with some assertions that may trouble some readers. God spoke to Moses mouth to mouth as with a friend. I strongly suspect that He must speak to others of us through dreams, visions and dark sayings not because we are so advanced in the things of the Spirit, but because we are so crippled that He can get through to us in no other way. The necessity of such means of communication is evidence of our fleshly dysfunction, not our advanced spirituality. When we yearn for mystical experiences such as dreams and visions, I fear we have placed the focus in the wrong place and cheated ourselves of the true gift. We have desired the means to the end rather than the end itself, the palliative rather than the cure. The king who wrote Ecclesiastes realized, "For in many dreams and in many words there is emptiness. Rather, fear God" (Ecclesiastes 5:7). *Jesus, teach me to be Your friend!*

PART 3

Training and Placement

10

THE NECESSITY
OF WILDERNESS SOJOURNS

The Charismatic Movement that swept through the mainline churches in the '60s and '70s carried an inherent and tragic flaw: its fascination with and focus on the gifts of the Spirit. Consequently, for most of my adult life the Body of Christ has been disproportionately impressed with giftedness at the expense of attention to issues of holiness, Christian character and wholeness. This has led to disastrous consequences. We have suffered tsunami waves of bad prophecy and have witnessed the fall of many famous leaders to sins of greed, dishonesty, relational dysfunction and sexual trespass. When the foundations are flawed, the building totters, and God must send His cleansing judgment.

In the days to come a new generation of leadership will emerge, one trained in hiddenness and purified in the crucible of brokenness. Wholeness and humility will be their hallmark. God must pour forth His power in the Western world as He has already been doing in so many poor and developing nations, but He will not do so apart from a foundation of cleansed and broken leadership who have been rendered functionally incapable of wielding the Lord's power for personal advantage.

One of the most direction-setting words I ever received from the Lord came when I was complaining—whining, actually—about how the Lord seemed to be blessing other churches with wild increase in spite of the sins that affected their leadership. At the same time He seemed to be holding those of us at New Song Fellowship back while He forced us to look at and deal with issues others seemed to be getting away with. I demanded to know why others were given grace while He kept us on such a short chain. The answer has never stopped resonating in my spirit: "My people cannot afford any more train wrecks." Over the years—and especially recently—the Western Church has suffered a large number of moral failures on the part of major ministry leaders in whom God's people placed their trust. Tens of thousands of Christians in my own city, for instance, no longer attend church because of betrayals and wounding suffered at the hands of broken leadership. I suspect the same is true in many other places. God was telling me that this must stop.

The new leadership about to emerge in the Body of Christ stands crushed, broken and humbled before Him. They can be entrusted with the treasures of heaven because they will neither usurp the glory of God nor abuse His people. They come with a pure word, uncolored by the brokenness and ambitions of men and women. They are not perfect—far from it. But love does cover a multitude of sins, and mercy truly triumphs over judgment (see 1 Peter 4:8 and James 2:13). We will be a people of love and mercy in humility but, to use a silly American figure of speech, we cannot get there from here. Our human nature, short of the cross, cannot sustain the power and love God wants to send.

God used a forty-year wilderness sojourn to refine faithlessness out of Israel. Wilderness suffering remains the path to glory.

Pathema

Pathema is a New Testament Greek word used to describe a particular kind of suffering, the *sine qua non* of high calling. One who has not passed through the valley of *pathema* cannot assume the high calling of God. In Philippians 3:10 Paul wrote that he had lost everything in order to gain Christ, "that I may know Him and the power of His resurrection and the fellowship of His *sufferings* [*pathema*], being conformed to His death" (emphasis mine). Jesus' suffering and death brought redemption, the cleansing of sin. When we say that we have died with Him, we express more than just a theological construct or a mere positional reality. Dying in union with Him can become a real form of suffering. As He conforms us to His death, the structures of sin embedded in our thought patterns and emotional makeup enter into a process of being crushed and broken.

But it does not end there. In verse 11 Paul wrote, "In order that I may attain to the resurrection from the dead." He spoke of the final bodily resurrection God promises at the end of the age, but I cannot believe he intended only that. Out of the crushing and death of our fleshly ways of thinking, feeling and doing comes a wonderful rising into the nature and character of Jesus.

First Peter 4 expresses a similar thought:

Therefore, since Christ has *suffered* in the flesh, arm yourselves also with the same purpose, because he who has *suffered* in the flesh has ceased from sin, so as to live the rest of the time in the flesh no longer for the lusts of men, but for the will of God.

verses 1–2, emphasis mine

The budding prophet of the Lord must arm himself or herself with the intention of suffering in such a way that personal desires, insecurities, needs, fears, judgments, strongholds and vulnerabilities are crushed and then swallowed up in Jesus. What rises in place of these things is a vessel consumed with desire for the will of God, resting in it and trusting Him for the goodness of it.

> I have been crucified with Christ; and it is no longer I who live, but Christ lives in me; and the life which I now live in the flesh I live by faith in the Son of God, who loved me and gave Himself up for me.

Galatians 2:20

My life for His!

No person of high calling escapes this process of dying. No person of high calling can afford to escape it. I grieve over the wreckage I have seen in those who rejected the process or bailed out before it could run its course, people who denied that their flesh had polluted their lives and ministries as deeply as it actually had. Those who persevere in brokenness and hold nothing back develop an aroma of sweetness about them and bear a healing anointing in which the people of God find needed rest and security.

All of us who are called to prophetic ministry must therefore experience *pathema*—the purifying wilderness. Without it there can be no realization of prophetic destiny. Character takes precedence over gifting. Along the way we can appear to be depressive and moody—and we are—but a Promised Land of blessing and peace lies on the other side of anguish.

Calling, Wilderness, Return

Immature prophetic people commonly and mistakenly assume that the anointing and power they feel coursing through them and the accurate words they deliver in the early days of their ministries constitute a prepaid ticket to the stars and that they will experience a steady rise into ever greater anointing without interruption. Nothing could be farther from the truth. Early success serves only to plant in us the promise of what God intends to do with us later in our development. All of us eventually will live out a pattern of early success and anointing followed by extended wilderness. Only when the wilderness has accomplished its intended work in our character will we be granted the fullness of the promise we received in the early days—our true destiny in Him. First comes calling and success, then exile and wilderness and finally return and fulfillment. No one bearing a prophetic destiny is exempt.

Joseph

The story of the unfolding of Joseph's prophetic destiny begins in Genesis 37. His early prophetic success came in the form of dreams that one day he would rule over his brothers as they bowed down before him. Filled with arrogance as his father's favorite son, he foolishly boasted to his brothers concerning the content of his dreams. Until this point in time he had enjoyed favor and ease, basking in his father's love and experiencing the power of the Lord's prophetic word, but the character flaw in him rendered him unusable as a genuine prophetic voice. In this first stage of the realization of his prophetic gift, God announced to Joseph what he was destined to do. He did not know that a wilderness of preparation and crushing for purification lay before him.

Offended at his pride and arrogance, Joseph's brothers sold him into slavery in Egypt, where stage two of his development as a prophet unfolded in exile and suffering. In Egypt the people he had served faithfully accused him falsely of a heinous crime. A lengthy and unjust imprisonment ensued before character changes took hold and his gift came to the attention of Pharaoh. With his character refined and humbled through suffering, he interpreted Pharaoh's dream and rose to the number two position of authority in Egypt. In that position many years later, he received his brothers in love and forgiveness and was able to sustain them in a time of famine as they came to bow before him and pay him obeisance in fulfillment of the prophetic dream. The pattern follows three stages: first, calling and success; second, an exile of suffering and character adjustment; and third, God grants the promised destiny.

How long does all this take? Some say the development of a true prophet takes 25 years. For a blockhead like me, it can require a fair bit longer. A lifetime would not be long enough.

David

In 1 Samuel the prophet anointed David king of Israel, but that did not prepare David for his destiny. Early battle successes aroused jealousy in the insane King Saul, who drove David into the wilderness to become the leader of a fugitive band of debtors, malcontents and misfits. Eventually King Saul died, and after years of wilderness alienation, false accusation and suffering, David ascended into his destiny to unite the tribes and become the greatest king Israel ever knew. Through his line came Jesus. I do not believe David could have entered his destiny without the changes wrought by his years of exile and suffering.

The pattern holds: calling, exile, return to destiny.

Saul Who Became Paul

After his dramatic conversion on the road to Damascus (see Acts 9), Saul immediately began to convince others zealously that this Jesus whom he had formerly persecuted was indeed the Son of God, the promised One. Acts 9:22 says, "But Saul kept increasing in strength and confounding the Jews who lived at Damascus by proving that this Jesus is the Christ." Early success in a clear calling!

But for the one in training for high calling, early successes must give way to the wilderness before true destiny can fully unfold. The time came when the Jews plotted to kill Saul, but his disciples learned of it and helped him escape the city through a hole in the wall. After a visit to Jerusalem, he went off to live in Tarsus as a tentmaker for fourteen years (see Galatians 2:1), a powerfully gifted man apparently sidelined for an extended period of time. Scripture reports nothing of him during those years until Barnabas came looking for him to aid in discipling the new believers at Antioch (see Acts 11:25). Only one of great gifting can truly understand the pain of being sidelined while the rest of the movement rushes by, seemingly leaving him behind. One must wonder how much of Paul's sense that he had suffered the loss of all things (see Philippians 3:8) was realized during those long years in Tarsus.

But the day arrived when Barnabas came looking. The great missionary journeys followed. Saul became Paul and surpassed Barnabas as the dominant member of the team.

Ultimately he became the chief arbiter of the foundational elements of our faith. Wilderness opened into a Promised Land when exile had accomplished its purpose.

Functions of the Wilderness

It should be obvious by now that the most foundational training a budding prophet must undergo has little to do with learning how to hear from God, how to interpret dreams or how to wield the power of heaven. It has everything to do with character development. Prophets in Bible times trained under older, more experienced prophets—not in order to reveal what the younger prophet was gifted to do but to expose to him what he could not do. It was a program designed to produce humility through menial tasks and failures. At the end, the young prophet would know both his weakness and his complete dependence on God.

Elijah, for example, appointed Elisha as his successor, but Elisha's calling began with servanthood, not gifting:

> So he returned from following him, and took the pair of oxen and sacrificed them and boiled their flesh with the implements of the oxen, and gave it to the people and they ate. Then he arose and followed Elijah and ministered to him.
>
> 1 Kings 19:21

Elisha would be a prophet of the Lord, but first he would be a servant.

The required level of servanthood went further even than this simple statement in 1 Kings 19. King Jehoshaphat sought the word of a prophet concerning war against the Moabites who had rebelled against him. He inquired, "'Is there not a prophet of the LORD here, that we may inquire of the LORD by him?' And one of the king of Israel's servants answered and said, 'Elisha the son of Shaphat is here, who used to pour water on the hands of Elijah'" (2 Kings 3:11). To pour water on the hands of another for washing was women's work in a time when it was considered a shattering humiliation for a man to be treated as a woman. The prophet in training would be broken, crushed and humbled long before he would be permitted to function as a prophet. We must understand our limitations and be trained in humility before we can be permitted to steward the living word of God.

Peter, the great apostle and leader of the Twelve, boasted that he would never abandon Jesus, that he would die with Him if need be (see Luke 22:33). In response, Jesus not only prophesied that Peter would deny Him three times that night, but He also included this: "Simon, Simon, behold, Satan has demanded permission to sift you like wheat; but I have prayed for you, that your faith may not fail; and you, when once you have turned again, strengthen your brothers" (Luke 22:31–32). Satan received permission to sift Peter to the point of exposing his weakness and failure. Jesus knew that Peter would be humiliated and broken at the point of his determination and pride. He would realize his weakness, but in that realization he would turn again in humility, now qualified and able to strengthen his brothers. Brokenness and failure had to come first. Power and authority flow best upon a riverbed of compassion born of a brokenness of spirit that results from the destruction of confidence in all things human.

For all the reasons I stated earlier in this book, we prophetic people are a messed-up, unbalanced, insecure segment of the Body of Christ. But we are coming into a period in the history of the Church and the world in which the role of the prophet is crucial, a time like no other when nothing will suffice for the character of those who lead but the true nature of Jesus. Jesus never abuses, never violates, never manipulates and never even exalts Himself despite His divinity. He lets His Father do that. In all these things we must reflect His nature.

The root of all spiritual abuse of others and all strongholds of control is unbelief in the true love the Father holds for us. It is insecurity at the deepest levels, and it originates invariably in a drive for self-validation and recognition. This produces selfish ambition that operates at the expense of those whom we have been sent to bless. This must die. Strongholds of self must be broken, and so our Lord sends us to the wilderness where flesh is crucified and unbelief is rooted out.

Wilderness Function #1: The Desperate Craving

Wilderness sufferings strip away every selfish ambition, every sense of personal accomplishment, every ability of the flesh to achieve, every sinful habit or stronghold of the heart until nothing remains but a desperate, urgent, holy hunger for the pure Spirit and presence of Jesus: "O God, You are my God; I shall seek You earnestly; my soul thirsts for You, my flesh yearns for You, in a dry and weary land where there is no water. Thus I have seen You in the sanctuary, to see Your power and Your glory" (Psalm 63:1–2).

Because David had been in the wilderness, whether figuratively, literally or both, he had been reduced to a singular yearning after the Lord. In and because of that focused yearning, he received a revelation of the power and glory of God: "Thus I have seen You in the sanctuary."

The wilderness makes you simple. It brings you to rest with your God. As he came thirsty from the desert, David, in all his kingly power, clung like a helpless child to His Lord: "My soul clings to You" (Psalm 63:8). The wilderness taught him that after all was said and done, he remained just a man, powerless and unimportant. Weak, defenseless and broken, his soul clung to the Lord, concerned no more with power, wisdom or place in the world. He yearned only for the embrace of his God.

Extended wilderness deprivation serves to reduce us to the only hunger that really matters. All true prophetic words flow not from the natural ability of the prophet to perceive and discern but from intimacy with God. The wilderness destroys all that stands at odds with that singular desire. With that hunger firmly established, the budding prophet becomes a safe and useful servant who will not abuse the flock of God or exalt self at their expense.

I cannot begin to explain how small I feel at this point in my life. Brought up in one of the leading families in the charismatic renewal, educated at one of the nation's best seminaries and now thirty years into a career in ministry, I stand empty, in possession of no gift or ability I ever thought I held. My personal wilderness has been a struggle with demonstrated gifting that produced little fruit. Constant questioning of the Lord's favor in my life has been one result. In fact, over the years I have been insulted, lied about and maligned at the very points of what I thought were my strongest gifts. Friends and trusted loved ones have betrayed me and left me alone to fight overpowering spiritual battles without human help. Some have even joined the other side. I think maybe I know a little of how Jesus felt when Peter denied Him three times, or when Judas gave Him up for crucifixion.

Unlike Jesus, however, I was arrogant, ambitious and in need of self-validation to medicate, cover and control my insecurities and fears. I could not begin to catalog the ways brokenness polluted my ministry as a pastor and the words

I thought were prophetic. I wounded many whom I loved, telling myself I was serving God when so much of it was really for me.

God sent an extended wilderness of failure, rejection and persecution that served to simplify and purify my hunger for Him as it gradually wore down the walls of my inner strongholds. As with Peter, He allowed Satan to sift me like wheat to purify in me a singular longing for Him. Then came the true revelation of the Father's love. "Thus I have seen You. . . ." I am entering a peace and rest I never before knew. In that peace, my Savior shares with me in ways He could never do before the wilderness did its work.

Wilderness Function #2: Testing

"You shall remember all the way which the LORD your God has led you in the wilderness these forty years, that He might humble you, testing you, to know what was in your heart, whether you would keep His commandments or not. He humbled you and let you be hungry, and fed you with manna which you did not know, nor did your fathers know, that He might make you understand that man does not live by bread alone, but man lives by everything that proceeds out of the mouth of the LORD."

Deuteronomy 8:2–3

Some of us would do well to examine ourselves to discover why we serve God. Is it for the thrill of the revelation? Is it because it somehow "works" for us, or because it produces prosperity, or perhaps because it feeds the sense of place and importance for which we so desperately long?

When the wilderness strips away these delusory motivations and then tests you to the core of yourself, when all that once made it easy to walk with God falls to rubble and your heart is broken, will you stand firm? Will you love Him when His love seems far from you? A prophet is destined to hear from God. If your wilderness consists of years of divine silence that cause pain so deep and intense that you feel you can bear it no longer, will you still be obedient? When years pass while unfulfilled promises accumulate, will you allow disappointment and emotional suffering to derail you, or will you stand in what you know you have been called to do? Will you remain firmly in Him whom you have committed yourself to serve? Will you allow pain to make you self-centered in your depression, or will you obediently keep giving to others, focusing your life outside of yourself no matter what the inner pressures might be? If you cannot stand with Him when everything seems wrong, how shallow and cheap will your devotion and service be in the midst of blessing and release?

You no longer ask, "Does obedience work?" In this testing, you learn to obey only because it is right to obey and for the sake of being with Jesus.

Here is a paradox. God will humiliate you in the very areas in which He plans to gift and bless you. I am a musician and songwriter. Today many who have come to our church to stay tell me that the worship music is one of the key reasons they came and stayed. Through all the years of wilderness, however, my music remained locked up and hidden away. In fact, in the first church I served after moving to Denver, other musicians mocked and ridiculed my style. Most doors seemed closed, but today I have eleven CDs to my credit and our church owns its own studio.

Integrity is crucial to me, but during my wilderness sojourn, it seemed that decisions were forced upon me in which no course of action could be found that did not compromise some commitment I had made. I was humbled and even humiliated that I was not even strong or wise enough to guard my integrity.

So you are called to be a prophet? No one wants to hear your words, and nothing you say comes to pass. Teaching is part of your gift mix? No one comes to your class. You write books? Who buys them? You turn to the world to find prosperity? Your department sets a sales record, but you could not sell a new car if it were free. Nothing works, and no one can explain why.

Prophetic people above all others must be reduced to a state in which we receive honor and humiliation, success and failure with equal gratitude because the wilderness has produced in us a singular hunger for the presence and love of Jesus. Nothing else matters.

Wilderness Function #3: Secure Identity

Wilderness testing, properly embraced, serves to establish a sense of identity as a son or daughter of God that cannot be easily threatened later. And prophetic people *will* be threatened. The threat usually centers on our sense of security—or lack of it—in who we are and what we have become in Jesus.

Jesus Himself came up from the waters of baptism and immediately "was led up by the Spirit into the wilderness to be tempted by the devil" (Matthew 4:1). Let us be clear: The Holy Spirit—not the devil—initiates wilderness sufferings. The devil may be involved but only by divine permission.

In confronting Jesus, Satan sought a window of vulnerability to exploit. He chose to seek insecurity and doubt in Jesus concerning His identity and therefore tested Him at the point of the most essential elements of His nature. As the Son of God, Jesus was God incarnate—fully God and fully man. On that foundation His entire ministry would be built, from making disciples and teaching the principles of heaven to dying for our sin and rising from the grave. If that foundation in identity could have been shaken, the entire purpose of God in Christ could have been thwarted.

This being understood, the heart of the temptation of Jesus can be found in Matthew 4:3, 6 in a question designed to cast doubt on His identity and security: *"If* You are the Son of God," then command the stones to become bread, or cast Yourself down and be caught by the angels. As the perfect Son of God, Jesus would be completely obedient to His Father, saying and doing nothing that did not originate in His Father, as He would later declare: "Truly, truly, I say to you, the Son can do nothing of Himself, unless it is something He sees the Father doing; for whatever the Father does, these things the Son also does in like manner" (John 5:19).

Jesus' answers to Satan's temptations defined and established His identity as the obedient One devoted to His Father alone. The test was not one Jesus would pass or fail, but rather it was something arranged by the Holy Spirit to affirm and strengthen Him in His sense of identity as God's Son. He would live only by His Father's words (see Matthew 4:4). He would not force a test on His Father and so violate the relationship (see verse 7). He would grant honor and worship only to His Father, no matter the price (see verse 10). These things formed the foundation of Jesus' earthly life and ministry and remain just as essential today for any who follow in His footsteps—most especially prophetic people.

I believe that Jesus emerged from His wilderness temptations affirmed and established in His own place and identity as the Son of God. He was settled in His mission to suffer obediently for us and was confirmed in the knowledge that He would rise to no ambition or cheap shortcut to glory that would endanger His relationship as the Son of His Father.

Many centuries prior to this, the nation of Israel suffered forty years of wandering in the wilderness to root out unbelief and disobedience until they knew who they were in relation to their God. With their identity as the people of God firmly established in faith, they were able to conquer and occupy the Promised Land.

I personally wasted many precious years not really understanding my own identity—doubting my chosenness. Old roots of rejection kept me from fully believing and experiencing the Lord's favor over me. As a result I built a huge fleshly edifice of personal achievement and ambition around myself to compensate for the absence of real trust and rest in who I was in Jesus. I even became abusive and manipulative as a leader in my efforts to maintain an outward appearance of success that would enable me to avoid facing my deep sense of rejection. The wilderness exposed and broke the stronghold of rejection, revealed my God to me, set my hunger in order and taught me who I am. Prophetic people can be deeply mired in roots of rejection that pollute their perception of the Lord's voice and the delivery of what they hear. We must learn in humility who He is and who we are in Him and then rest firmly in it.

Wilderness Function #4: Rest

"And He said to them, 'Come away by yourselves to a secluded place and rest a while'" (Mark 6:31). Jesus and the disciples were forced to delay their rest because the people pursued them and got there first, but Jesus nevertheless sought out secluded places of wilderness. Luke 5:16 says, "But Jesus Himself would often slip away to the wilderness and pray." The wilderness for Israel is the paradigmatic place of meeting with God, sometimes a place of temptation and suffering and sometimes a place of rest and prayer.

If our modern wilderness is a figurative place of loneliness and redemptive suffering, then God intends it also to be a place to rest and find Him. We must learn to peacefully embrace solitude and loneliness—no one else will truly understand what we are going through—and plumb the depths of hunger and thirst for Him. To rest is to yield to this place of deprivation into which the Holy Spirit has led us, to surrender to the wilderness and allow it to do its work.

Jesus wants more from us than our service and obedience. He longs for *us*, and paradoxically He will risk the loss of us in order to fully gain us.

I hurt so badly I desperately wanted to quit but could not bring myself to seriously entertain the idea. Unable to rest in and embrace the suffering, how many actually give up the calling? "For many are called, but few are chosen" (Matthew 22:14). Because of the pain, thirst and loneliness, how many finally cut short the process before sighting the promise of the Jordan shore?

In the wilderness it can seem that you have lost your ministry and will never regain it. I recall wondering sarcastically how the Lord thought He would be glorified if my church collapsed. I truly feared it might! Why was He doing this to me? The wilderness taught me that if He must choose between the ministry and me, He will choose me every time. He loves me that much. God can raise up ministries with a word, but a man or a woman is a precious and beloved child for whom He died. I choose to rest in the wilderness when I am thrust into it. It is an indispensable source of life to me and might be said to be an essential second home for the prophetic person.

A bit of the wilderness lingers in my heart always, like an echo of a memory I dare not forget. Its presence reminds me who I am and who I am not. It teaches me wisdom and tethers me to humility, that quality of character I have always found so stubbornly elusive. The wilderness reminds me of my own weakness and of God's strength, that He alone is my Provider. It sharpens and purifies my hunger for the presence of my precious Lord. The Holy Spirit still takes me to the wilderness whenever I wander off track or forget some essential lesson of life, ministry or relationship with Him. Sometimes it is just that He knows I must go deeper in my changes and that the wilderness is the only way to reach that goal. To rest in the wilderness is to treasure it despite the pain it can bring.

Ministry itself can be a place of rest when the wilderness has borne its fruit. Having been overshadowed by the sovereignty of an all-powerful God, self-motivated efforts of the flesh cease. In recent years I have been learning how to rest in the Lord while ministering. As a result my body may tire, but my spirit and my emotional state draw continual refreshment. I am increasingly aware that it is not "me" being poured out.

More importantly, after the wilderness the ministry is no longer rooted in my gifting. It was never my gifting anyway. That was a fleshly conceit. The gifts are "the gifts of the Spirit," which means they belong to Him, not me. Neither is it "my" anointing. Anointing comes by the Spirit of God and belongs to Him. No matter how talented or gifted I might be, without Him it all amounts to nothing. Accordingly I cannot own the prophetic word. It was never mine to own.

Prophetic people often exhibit significant natural psychic abilities and mistakenly think that everything they see and sense through these natural abilities must be of God. We have a tendency to take ownership and pride in these gifts and abilities. The wilderness defeats these misconceptions. It roots our natural abilities firmly in Him, under His authority. No good fruit can come from anything not rooted in Him. "Apart from Me you can do nothing" (John 15:5). Neglect of this truth makes the erstwhile prophet a dangerous tool in the hands of the enemy rather than a carrier of the word of God.

The wilderness is therefore a place where God blesses by not blessing. You learn not what you *can* do but what you *cannot* do until you come to rest in Him. Remember that Joseph received the Lord's word through dreams, but in his arrogance and pride he misinterpreted and misused those dreams to belittle and enrage his brothers. He failed at his calling and was sold off into his personal wilderness of suffering and character formation. God sustained him through it all but allowed him to experience enough pain to bring about the changes that had to be made. God sustains us in the wilderness while He holds back the promise until the changed character of the budding prophet can bear the weight of the gift in rest.

Wilderness Function #5: Restoration

"Therefore, behold, I will allure her, bring her into the wilderness and speak kindly to her. Then I will give her her vineyards from there, and the valley of Achor as a door of hope. And she will sing there as in the days of her youth, as in the day when she came up from the land of Egypt."

Hosea 2:14–15

When God sets out to build a great work, He digs a deep hole for the foundation. The greater the work, the deeper the hole! Sin is judged and cleansed. In the embracing of redemptive suffering, strongholds of thought, behavior and emotion that were raised up against the true knowledge of God are broken, transformed and brought under the blood of Jesus. The foundation goes deep enough and strong enough to build upon it. In the heat of the cleansing fire, character solid enough to bear the weight of power and blessing is forged until the time comes when our Lord deems us safe to steward the gift of destiny.

Our Lord is always more concerned with character formation than with building great ministries for us. He is ever more concerned with what adversity produces in us than with delivering us from it. In my own wilderness the Lord began to grant me the realization of a list of character changes for which I had longed all my life. He restored me to Himself when I had become lost in fear, striving, ambition and control. Most of all He restored me to myself.

I once had control of a hard and emotionless exterior, but recently my eldest daughter teased me: "Dad, you cry about everything!" True! I have learned to be vulnerable—to stop and smell the roses, as the saying goes. A prophet's heart must be tender for the Lord and tender for His people. The wilderness taught me this as the Father used it to restore me to my true self. I do not believe it could have come about in any other way.

Wilderness Function #6: Preparation

A voice is calling, "Clear the way for the LORD in the wilderness; make smooth in the desert a highway for our God. Let every valley be lifted up, and every mountain and hill be made low; and let the rough ground become a plain, and the rugged terrain a broad valley; then the glory of the LORD will be revealed, and all flesh will see it together; for the mouth of the LORD has spoken."

Isaiah 40:3–5

We all long for the Lord to come into our lives with power. Most of us fail to realize that His coming requires a significant period of preparation and a wilderness of deprivation.

In the ancient Near East, roads were built only for the king and were repaired only when the king announced an impending visit. Our King is coming, but we must prepare for Him. The bumps must be smoothed out of His highway, the potholes filled and the surface leveled.

At least in part, this is accomplished as wilderness reduces us to that singular longing where nothing will satisfy but God alone and in which we have given up seeking fulfillment from any other source. Being with Him becomes more important than success or recognition. Personal need and fear no longer defile or impede the ministry at any level. Without this preparatory wilderness there can be no fulfillment of promise and no unfolding of divinely ordained destiny. The road has not been made ready.

For those who embrace the wilderness and let it work its work, who seek healing when the wilderness has exposed the need, I can promise a wonderful increase of intimacy with God. Love will flow. Heaven will open. Truth will unfold and God's people will be fed. Restoration and return do follow after exile.

Wilderness Dangers

Suffering often magnifies temptation, increasing the opportunity for error. I list here some common errors guaranteed to prolong or even derail the process of training and refining.

Danger #1: Anger and Bitterness

In the midst of my own wilderness—when my ministry was failing, my wife and children were coming under assault from outside and even my own parents and siblings seemingly abandoned me in times of crisis—I worked hard at denying my anger. I did it because I understood that anger would accomplish nothing and because I had been schooled in control as a child. Knowing that emotional freedom was essential to my calling and to the welfare of those I loved, I wanted to embrace the pain, hurt and alienation as deeply and fully as possible, even as I struggled with my anger over the unfairness of it. I longed for the fruit of the wilderness to manifest sooner so that I could exit that painful season of my life as quickly as God would allow.

But in spite of my control mechanisms and denials, I was indeed angry—and more so than I had ever realized. All the accusations, rejections, setbacks and losses did not seem fair. Was I really so wicked as to be worthy of all this? And did God really expect me to embrace this relentless pain with no bitterness? The answer was yes. It became clear to me that as long as I had the energy to be angry with God over the losses He was allowing in my life, then I had some distance yet to go. We must seek God's grace to surrender to the process without bitterness.

Someone once asked me, "Can I make it shorter?" I replied, "No, but you can make it longer"—by fighting the pain and resisting the process. How easily we can turn to blaming God for the setbacks and heartaches, disappointments and betrayals!

Personally, I finally burned out on judging God for His dealings with me. Anger consumes energy, and I was fresh out of anything that looked like strength. In the desert, with Egypt not far behind them, Israel was an angry people until the wilderness burned it out of them. They confronted every new obstacle not as an opportunity to believe and rest in the Lord for a miracle but as an occasion to grumble and complain against God and against Moses. It mattered little how many times God rescued them or how clearly and faithfully He sustained them. Sin has a life of its own until God crucifies it.

Wounding by the Lord's hand is a gift of love designed to prepare us for the wonder of our destiny by refining and changing our character. Properly embraced, wounding takes out the bumps in the Lord's road and prepares us for the coming of the real presence of God. In the end, genuine faith takes root and we minister from a base of true rest in Him.

Danger #2: Loss of Faith

How ironic it is that the very thing sent to seek out and destroy stumbling blocks to real faith could actually result in the erosion of it! At the depths of my wilderness purification I knew for certain that the favor of the Lord as I had understood and desired it did not rest on me. Worse, I knew that nothing I could do would serve to restore it. I could repent for being arrogant, but that would not make me humble. I could understand the roots of my control mechanisms and my domination of others, but that would not conquer the strongholds that had grown from these things. I could invest so many hours in the ministry that my body failed in fatigue, but none of these things would bring the favor for which I longed—at least not until what needed to break had been broken and what needed to be conquered had been surrendered.

The faith problem surfaced when the process had nearly run its course, when character changes had taken root and the Promised Land was at hand. I found that I could not readily transition out of the wilderness to believe the Lord for the promises. The wilderness mentality can become a stronghold of its own and can prevent your entry into destiny as readily as can character flaws. I was pretty sure God did not have a heart to bless me and that He never would again. My theology told me otherwise, but my heart could not receive it.

This kind of thinking often can be identified by the language it produces: "God will never . . . " "It will always be this way." "This always happens." You have lived with wilderness deprivation and suffering for so long that it has affected your habitual thought patterns until you can no longer see past them. The wilderness is the necessary preparation for high calling, but wilderness unbelief and wilderness despair can render you incapable of recognizing, receiving or believing the promise when at last it comes.

In my case, one of the roots that needed to be exposed was an ungodly belief that I would always be forced to fight my battles alone without help. Believing he was doing the right thing to make me strong, my father trained me that way as a child—"Fight your own battles, son!"—until it hardened into a stronghold of bitter expectation. I found it impossible to believe that Father God would back me up or fight for me, even when I was doing His work. Fear, striving, domination and control grew from that root, and I exhausted myself with it. No prophet of God can afford to carry that kind of brokenness into the ministry. Just picture Elijah facing 450 prophets of Baal in a contest of power, convinced that he was on his own and that Father God would not back him up! Elijah had to know the truth and be rested in it—and so did I.

When the wilderness drew to a close, therefore, wilderness thinking had to end, as well. I therefore began to seek healing with the help of those who could point the way. Here is the paradox. In love, my Father God disciplined me in the wilderness by leaving me to fight more difficult battles on my own than I could possibly bear in my flesh. He did this precisely so that I would break and so that, in the breaking, unbelief would be refined out of my character. I had to fail before I could succeed. When that purpose had been accomplished, He restored visible favor over my life and began to entrust me with destiny. All of it, every part and parcel, had been an expression of His favor, but at the end I had to make a deliberate choice to believe it.

Danger #3: Apostasy

Under the pressure, pain and loneliness of the wilderness, how many of us have said to ourselves, *That's enough! God doesn't keep His promises! This doesn't work!* and seriously considered opting for a lesser level of discipleship, bailing out of church and otherwise abandoning the practice of our faith as we had understood it? "For many are called, but few are chosen" (Matthew 22:14). Could this be why? In the Old Testament, Job made a decision the rest of us would do well to study and emulate: "Though He slay me, I will hope in Him" (Job 13:15).

Danger #4: Rebellion

When I was just five or six years old, my mother punished me for trying to carry the baby without adult supervision—something I was not yet grown-up enough to do safely. She sent me to my room for a period of time that I felt was unjust and excessively lengthy. Angered, I decided to climb out the window, climb down the ivy vines that clung to the side of our brick home and run away. Being a true bonehead, about six blocks away I realized I was not going to get far without my shoes, and so I returned home, hoping to sneak back into the house without being seen. Of course, my mother met me at the door wearing a face that told me life as I knew it had just ended.

Wilderness sojourns can cause us to feel as though we are being unjustly punished and sentenced to forms and lengths of exile out of proportion to what we really deserve. This, of course, is a fallacy, but in our immaturity this sense of injustice can lead us to engage in forms of rebellion that tend to defeat the purposes of God and lengthen the time we must spend in the searing heat and loneliness of the desert.

Unfortunately, in times like these some of us become vulnerable to various forms of immorality in which we indulge simply for the sake of rebellion. *You haven't satisfied me, Lord, so I'll just go look at some pornography! At least there I can feel something!* I often thought, *Why can't I just go get roaring drunk like anybody else?* I could not. I knew that. But rebellion can carry a sweet allure under certain circumstances.

Or we can pursue ministries in the name of the Lord when the truth is that we are doing it in rebellion in an attempt to escape the heat of the desert. For instance, God had set up my church and my ministry in Idaho to deteriorate in the exact way it did. Failure was an essential part of my wilderness training to get at the "stuff" in me that needed to be changed. God had called me to leave northern Idaho, but I did not want to hear it, so in rebellion I planted a satellite congregation in the Spokane Valley twenty minutes away. For a number of months I led two services each Sunday, one in Post Falls, Idaho, and one across the state line in Spokane, Washington. I expected the Spokane congregation to flourish. I expected to drink the elixir of success and be validated in my true giftedness. Of course, it failed. God refuses to bless any plans but His own.

There is no way around the wilderness. You can get over it only by humbly and obediently going through it.

Danger #5: Disobedience

What if I had quit the ministry to escape the pain? I wanted to! It was in the midst of the wilderness that my Lord told me the way to transform the church and lead it out of the sickness of self-focus was to preach nothing but Jesus Christ and Him crucified. Had I refused, none of the wonderful changes that have happened to us at New Song Fellowship in Denver, Colorado, would have occurred. Our outreach to Native Americans would never have developed. There would have been no food bank, no neighborhood distributions of clothing or other goods to the poor, no counseling department restoring lives, no proliferation of love and healing to all those who have found it with this ministry.

At one point my Lord commanded me to publicly apologize and make amends to the elders of the church I served for abusing them in my brokenness. What if my pride or the anticipated pain of exposing myself in that way had led me to refuse? Blessings would have been lost, and character changes would have been delayed. My wilderness sojourn would have lengthened.

Danger #6: Turning to Other Powers

When the Philistines threatened to overwhelm him, Saul turned to other powers as he visited the medium and called up the spirit of Samuel for help (see 1 Samuel 28). His relationship with the Lord stood broken because of rebellion and disobedience. In his despair and need for help, he sought out a medium, a practice clearly condemned everywhere in the Law. Times of wilderness can leave us feeling as Saul felt, overwhelmed and alone, abandoned by God. During such seasons we can be tempted to turn to spiritual methods and resources clearly forbidden to us, although they may appear to be Christian at the time.

193

Other powers might include domination and control, management by intimidation, fleshly strength and talent or compromise with New Age techniques for generating spiritual experiences. The Lord sent me to the wilderness in part by allowing decline in my ministry. Facing the same scenario, I have seen men and women of God refuse to embrace wilderness suffering and then turn to lies and deceptions in order to hold the crumbling "empire" together. Dishonest fund-raising approaches and false promises become part of the system of avoidance, together with blaming and abusing others for the decline.

Driven by desperation and not yet broken, all of us are capable of turning to any number of "other powers" in an attempt to end the pain. This only prolongs the process. The only way "out" is "through." The difference between redemptive suffering and misery is found in whether you embrace the experience or waste time fighting it.

A sardonic smile on his face, a friend of mine once told me, "The more you complain, the longer God lets you live." He who has an ear, let him hear. The prophet without a wilderness behind him or her is only kidding himself or herself.

11

STILL DEEPER IN THE DARK NIGHT OF THE SOUL

The higher the calling, the deeper the hole required for the foundation. Yes, I have already said that. No, we have not yet plumbed the depths of that subject.

I really would like to avoid this chapter. In my training I have visited pits of darkness that I do not care to revisit, even in distant memory. But these pits are the price that must be paid for certain kinds of calling and destiny.

It often seems to me that "prophetic" is the latest thing everyone in the charismatic movement wants to be. As one who has traveled long on that road, I can say only that those who aspire to prophetic calling need to rethink their goals. No one fully informed and in his or her right mind would choose this path unless the call of God proved irresistible. Moses argued with the Lord, pleading for another to be sent, until "the anger of the LORD burned against Moses" (Exodus 4:14). Jeremiah resisted his calling, protesting, "Alas, Lord GOD! Behold, I do not know how to speak, because I am a youth" (Jeremiah 1:6), and the Lord rebuked him for it. I believe these prophets understood instinctively what it would cost them.

The dark night of the soul is a step beyond the wilderness. More than in the wilderness, the dark night of the soul seems to be void of the Lord's presence or blessing. Disaster piles upon disaster with no relief in sight. Nothing works. You fail in all you try. In the dark night of the soul, you plead, *Lord, if I hurt any worse, if one more thing comes down on me, I'll break!* and the Lord seems to reply, *Right! Isn't that the point?* At least in the wilderness I could find a sweet place of solitude with the Holy Spirit in the embracing of it. In the dark night of the soul, no such place can be found. Internally all is loneliness and suffering, while externally the womb of ministry seems closed and barren.

The Promise in the Barren Womb

Let us therefore establish hope before exploring the fullness of the dark night. From the beginning God has brought redemptive destiny out of the barren womb. Sarah waited well into her old age before conceiving the gift of Isaac, and even then Abraham had to show himself willing to sacrifice the son of promise on which his entire destiny depended (see Genesis 22) so that there could be no personal or fleshly ownership of the purposes of God.

Barrenness devastated Rachel, Jacob's wife, until the birth of Joseph. In joy she cried out, "God has taken away my reproach" (Genesis 30:23). Remember that cry! It will be important later as we explore the effects of the dark night of the soul. God will finally take away reproach. Had it not been for Joseph and the fulfillment of his destiny, the line of Abraham might have ended in famine.

Childless Hannah pled with the Lord, believing she had been forgotten by Him (see 1 Samuel 1), and like Abraham she surrendered her son to the Lord as soon as she had weaned him, owning nothing for herself. Samuel grew up to become both priest and prophet, anointing and commissioning kings.

In the New Testament, Elizabeth, childless in her old age, conceived and bore John the Baptist. Sometime during the first five joyous months of her pregnancy she exclaimed, "This is the way the Lord has dealt with me in the days when He looked with favor upon me, to take away my disgrace among men" (Luke 1:25). Her son became the forerunner for Jesus, the first prophetic voice to arise in four hundred years!

It would be exceedingly difficult for any who have not experienced barrenness to comprehend what it means to a woman—especially what it would have meant to a woman in Bible times. Every agony a barren couple suffers today would have been magnified by ancient Near Eastern attitudes in a culture that placed a woman's entire worth in her ability to bear children. Rachel spoke of it as reproach, the mocking condemnation of others who cannot or will not understand your suffering. Elizabeth expressed it as disgrace, a sense of shame and failure that cut to the core of her sense of self. People thought a barren woman had been rejected and cursed by God. *Despair* would be a weak word for what these women felt as the years passed.

Yet over and over again God causes redemptive history and the destiny of His people to unfold out of the agony of the closed womb, the delayed promise, the ministry that stubbornly refuses to grow, so that the pregnancy that brings eternal fruit is clearly the Lord's and not of human origin. The very thing men regard as rejected becomes the agent of Israel's greatest blessing.

Similarly the dark night of the soul is a closed womb and a delayed promise. The most gifted and talented of us find ourselves absolutely barren—and not just barren but mocked, accused, discounted and rejected because of it. And like the opening of the closed womb, the end of the dark night of the soul brings eternal fruit that is clearly the Lord's and not of human origin. Like Abraham and Hannah in their willingness to give up their children, we who have suffered the dark night have been made ready to surrender everything so that we take no personal ownership of the blessing, anointing and fulfillment. It is all about the Kingdom of God and not about us.

If the wilderness served to adjust character, the dark night of the soul breaks the spirit. For this reason we experience the dark night at much deeper levels. People who are merely prophetic, as opposed to holders of prophetic office, might get away with a simple wilderness experience, but at some point the true prophetic officeholder will be plunged into a black hole of suffering and abandonment that he or she can neither comprehend nor bear up under. Wilderness pales by comparison.

Because the Body of Christ has no effective grid through which to process what appears to be senseless suffering, the dark night of the soul is often filled with Job's comforters who heap condemnation and judgment upon the sufferer in the name of loving confrontation. Reproach. Disgrace. The barren womb. But in the end redemption comes. Destiny unfolds. Power is released.

In the late seventeenth and early eighteenth centuries Madame Guyon, who lived in France and was persecuted and imprisoned by the Church, described the dark night of the soul in terms I can scarcely improve upon:

There comes a time in the believer's life when the Lord withdraws the joy. He will seemingly withdraw the graces. At the same time, the Christian may also find himself in a period of persecution—persecution, no less, than that coming from Christians in religious authority. Further, he may find much difficulty in his home or private life. He may also be experiencing great difficulties with his health. Somewhere there will be a great deal of pain or other losses too numerous to mention. The believer may also be undergoing experiences which he feels are totally unique to himself. Other Christians, in whom he has put his trust, may forsake him and mistreat him. He may feel that he has been unjustly treated. He will feel this toward men, and he will feel it toward his God, for—in the midst of all this other pain and confusion—it will seem that God, too, has left him! Even more believers give up the journey when the Lord seems to have forsaken them in the spirit and left their spirits dead—while the world and all else is crashing in on them, friends forsaking them, and great suffering and pain abounding everywhere in their lives. . . . But the true Land of Promise always lies beyond a vast wasteland. Promise is found only on the far side of a desert. . . . When you can go beyond that place and, not seeing your Lord, believe He is there by the eyes of faith alone; when you can walk further and further into Christ when there are no senses, no feelings, not even the slightest registration of the presence of God; when you can sit before Him when everything around you and within you seems to be either falling apart or dead; and when you can come before your Lord without question and without demand, serene in faith alone, and there, before Him, worship Him without distraction, without a great deal of consciousness of self and with no spiritual sense of Him, then will the test of commitment begin to be established. Then will begin the true journey of the Christian life.

Jeanne Guyon, *Final Steps in Christian Maturity*, Jacksonville, FL: SeedSowers, 1985, used by permission

The Dark Night in Psalm 88

Is such an experience described in Scripture, or are we reading into the Word something human beings have experienced in order to glorify an experience with which God has nothing to do? I have sometimes spoken of Psalm 88 as the only psalm in the Bible with not a shred of clear hope, a psalm expressing an agony so deep the author could see no end of it. But while it expresses undiluted desperation and despair, it also contains crucial nuggets of wisdom for successfully coming through and out of the dark night.

Verses 1–3

"O LORD, the God of my salvation, I have cried out by day and in the night before You. Let my prayer come before You; Incline Your ear to my cry! For my soul has had enough troubles, and my life has drawn near to Sheol." In the dark night of the soul, you suffer from emotional agony overload. You feel as if you have absorbed as much as you can absorb and that even one more ounce of suffering would cause a breakdown. You know you are dying inside, and you feel helpless to stop it.

Verse 4

"I am reckoned among those who go down to the pit; I have become like a man without strength." This is where reproach from others begins. Observers, confused and frightened by what they see happening to you, conclude that you must be cursed by God somehow and that if you are cursed, then you must be deserving of the curse. The pressure of suffering from within combined with the condemnation of others from without saps strength. You find yourself physically, emotionally and spiritually broken, weakened in every way.

Verse 5

"Forsaken among the dead, like the slain who lie in the grave, whom You remember no more, and they are cut off from Your hand." The psalmist felt as though God had forgotten him. His sense of the presence of the Lord had vanished.

Toward the end of a long, personal dark night of the soul, I traveled to Toronto year after year at the height of the revival at the Toronto Airport Christian Fellowship, desperately hoping for a touch from God, but as people fell, shook and laughed all around me, I felt absolutely nothing. Others prayed for me, and they themselves fell under the power of the anointing they said was coming down on me, but I sensed none of it. Every time I went there I felt so rejected and fell into such depression that my wife threatened to refuse to make the trip with me anymore. The pain of the loss of His presence passed description. Years later God did meet me in Toronto in a dramatic and renewing encounter, but the early years were difficult.

Verse 6

"You have put me in the lowest pit, in dark places, in the depths." Here is a true statement of faith. The psalmist plainly understood that this was God's doing. I, too, knew that my own sense of suffering and abandonment originated with Him. In the wilderness I understood what needed changing and could embrace what God was doing in the adjustment of my character, but this experience passed beyond my ability to creatively deal with it. At the time it seemed senseless and without purpose.

Verse 7

"Your wrath has rested upon me, and You have afflicted me with all Your waves. Selah." Nameless and baseless guilt can take root during the dark night of the soul. Despite what I knew to be theologically correct, there were moments when I cried out, "Why do You hate me?" because it was the truth of how I felt. Wave after wave of rejection and disaster roared over and through me with little or no time to recover in between. My church was dying. Trusted friends were falsely imprisoned for the murder of a child. My personal finances were disastrously audited by the Internal Revenue Service. The surrogate sons in my family's ministry were maneuvering me out as a perceived threat. My own son suffered daily attacks at school just for being my son. My daughters would have been sexually assaulted had they not had the sense to run home.

There was more—too much to tell here. It all happened in the space of a year, but the deepest agony was that I lost all sense of the Lord's love and touch. Like the psalmist, I felt I was a man who had lost his footing in the surf so that the waves rolled him over and over in helplessness, filling his mouth and eyes with sand while he choked on saltwater.

Verse 8

"You have removed my acquaintances far from me; You have made me an object of loathing to them; I am shut up and cannot go out." Although the psalmist attributed the removal of his friends to the hand of God, I know from experience that in fact no one could stand to be around him anymore. When suffering runs so deep and seems so pointless, others cannot make sense of it. What people cannot understand frightens them, and what frightens them causes them to withdraw. The dark night is an experience you can share with no one. You walk it alone.

The stress of suffering and loss had taken such a toll that the psalmist could no longer even bring himself to venture out in public. There were times in my life when so much had gone so wrong for so long—times when I was so alone and so condemned—that I could not control the trembling in my hands and had to stay home, working from my home office as I hid from the world.

Verse 9

"My eye has wasted away because of affliction; I have called upon You every day, O LORD; I have spread out my hands to You." Here is a major key. No matter how he felt, no matter how distant God seemed, the psalmist prayed. This was Madame Guyon's testimony, and it is mine, as well. I determined by force of will to reach out to God in a disciplined and daily prayer life and to press into Him ever more deeply, even when there seemed to be no respite from pain and no sense of His presence in the midst of it. I did it not because of any holiness or strength inherent in myself, but because to fail to do so appeared to be an unacceptable alternative bearing consequences worse than those I already bore.

Verse 10

"Will You perform wonders for the dead? Will the departed spirits rise and praise You? Selah." Relentless, senseless pain and suffering reduced him to sarcasm, as if to say, "You love to be praised! How will I do that when I am dead? You're killing me! Bad move, Lord!" Eventually the agony of the long dark night burned this kind of anger out of me, but until then I spent a lot of time seething.

Verses 11–12

"Will Your lovingkindness be declared in the grave, Your faithfulness in Abaddon? Will Your wonders be made known in the darkness? And Your righteousness in the land of forget-fulness?" More sarcasm. It is legal! Be honest with God about your feelings! He forbids only unfaithfulness and apostasy.

Verse 13

"But I, O LORD, have cried out to You for help, and in the morning my prayer comes before You." Here is the key once more. No matter how dark the night or how distant God may seem, you must faithfully press into His presence in prayer, no matter whether you perceive a response or not. Faithfulness keeps you in position to receive when the time comes for the Lord to manifest His presence once more. Those who abandon Him or turn away in times like these may find themselves out of position when He appears.

Further, apostasy of any kind cuts short the changes in your spirit that the long dark night is designed to bring about. Faithfulness pleases God, but the bigger issue is not the performance of faithfulness. Speaking figuratively, the bigger issue is that if you are not in the shower when the water comes on, then you cannot get wet. Faithful prayer keeps you in position, changing and being cleansed. Serve God, therefore, and pursue your ministry faithfully. Keep listening. Keep worshiping. Remain in fellowship, no mat-ter how painful it may seem. Choose to walk by faith even when blinded.

Verse 14

"O LORD, why do You reject my soul? Why do You hide Your face from me?" We keep coming back to rejection issues. The prophet of God must not be motivated or pol-luted by rejection issues. Rejection issues lead to attempts at acceptance and to a desire to be seen as powerful and important. Always this takes away from others, diminishing them and minimizing their gifts in order to inflate self. This need therefore pollutes the ministry of the word of God. The dark night exposes and burns away rejection.

Verse 15

"I was afflicted and about to die from my youth on; I suffer Your terrors; I am overcome." We call it the "long" dark night of the soul because it is indeed a long time of darkness. The psalmist had experienced this almost from childhood. I understand because I, too, felt afflicted in this way from an early age. Many prophetic people can testify to similar histories. In the first chapter of this book, I wrote of the overly serious nature of many prophetic people. This is one cause.

Verses 16–17

"Your burning anger has passed over me; Your terrors have destroyed me. They have surrounded me like water all day long; they have encompassed me altogether." Fear can be a constant companion in the dark night. From where will the next blow come? The next devastating rejection? The next disaster? The psalmist felt as though he were drowning, overcome by terrors he could no longer control. Stated simply, "Been there. Done that." Plagued with these fears, you struggle with shame and embarrassment over such a failure of faith, but no matter how hard you try, you cannot stop it. Paradoxically, God is burning unbelief out of you by allowing it to run out of control. At the end, faith will be established in the kind of divine rest that is so essential in the life and ministry of the prophet, but at this point you cannot imagine how that could possibly be.

Verse 18

"You have removed lover and friend far from me; my acquaintances are in darkness." Loneliness loomed so large that the psalmist felt compelled to restate it. Friends and acquaintances, especially those infected with the religious spirit, try to help with hurtfully inaccurate analyses of your problem, bad advice and cheap theology. When you cannot drink from the fountain of their "wisdom," most pull away with judgments and even condemnation on their hearts and lips. Because you are not much fun to be around, friendships erode, but through it all, cling to the knowledge that the hand of God is moving you into the deepest and most holy forms of brokenness before Him. Primary intimacy with Him, as opposed to primary intimacy with others, is the reward. All true prophetic words flow from intimacy with God.

Nine Purposes for the Dark Night of the Soul

In retrospect I see clearly and with gratitude the purposes of God in plunging me into the depths of the dark night of the soul. In the midst of it, however, I was blind. I hope that the following list eases the way for others by providing a foundation in understanding.

Purpose #1: Abandonment of Hope of Personal Reward

"Which of you, having a slave plowing or tending sheep, will say to him when he has come in from the field, 'Come immediately and sit down to eat'? But will he not say to him, 'Prepare something for me to eat, and properly clothe yourself and serve me while I eat and drink; and afterward you may eat and drink'? He does not thank the slave because he did the things which were commanded, does he? So you too, when you do all the things which are commanded you, say, 'We are unworthy slaves; we have done only that which we ought to have done.'"

Luke 17:7–10

The first purpose of the dark night of the soul is *to bring about abandonment of any hope of personal reward for loving or serving God*. This is not to say that God does not reward His servants. He most certainly does, as Scripture amply promises and testifies. The point is that it must be sufficient for us to have done as our Lord has commanded regardless of the outcome. Our love must be so focused, simple and pure that obedience becomes its own reward.

Prophetic people can be inundated by the praises of men, the satisfaction and even pride of fulfilled words, positions of influence and a nearly endless list of other sorts of positive reinforcement. Over time this system of rewards can assume an unhealthy place of importance in the life and ministry of the prophet. I wonder, for instance, how Jeremiah would have fared if the need for reward had not been substantially laid to rest in his life? He brought a hard word to Israel for which the praises of men came few and far between. People mocked and taunted. At one point his obedience got him thrown into an empty cistern and nearly left to die (see Jeremiah 38). The prophet cannot serve for personal reward at any level. He or she must serve for love alone. As long as any degree of need for personal reward or recognition motivates our service, that desire pollutes our ministry and colors our words. We must pursue our calling from a base of rest in the Lord, not from the labor of our own works. The hope of personal reward leads directly to fleshly effort.

Purpose #2: Exposure and Purification of Defects

The second purpose of the dark night of the soul is *to expose and purify defects by breaking them*. "For I know that nothing good dwells in me, that is, in my flesh; for the willing is present in me, but the doing of the good is not" (Romans 7:18). It would be a fatal mistake for the prophet to believe that because of his or her gifting—or for any other reason—he or she is basically a good person who somehow got broken and simply needs to be fixed by Jesus for the hidden wonder of his or her true self to emerge. The truth is that we are sinners to the core who must be crucified and raised with Jesus in order to live.

The dark night of the soul stripped me of any sense of personal virtue. I have never recovered it and I really do not care to. I now wear the righteousness of Jesus. How could anything in me compare with that?

As my church in Idaho began to die, I protested to the Lord that I wanted only to affect the community for Him. Why was this unjust thing happening to righteous me?

Yes, but you also wanted to have the largest church in town so that you would feel personally validated and important.

I cried, "Lord, I just wanted to preach Your word with power so as to turn the hearts of people to You!"

Yes, but you also wanted to impress them with your gifting and bask in their praises at how deep and profound you were, came the rebuke.

"I just wanted them to be faithful to You!" I cried in justification for dominating, controlling and manipulating. He rebuffed that one, as well. It was time to expose my unholy need to see bodies in seats in greater numbers so that I would feel affirmed and successful. By the time He was through with me, I stood devastated at the realization of my jealousy of other leaders who appeared more successful than I did, of my ambitions, insecurities, judgments, hatreds, lack of love and utter depravity. "Nothing good dwells in me," began to make more sense to me than I had ever imagined it could.

Like the apostle Paul, the prophet must despair of and despise every sense of self-goodness. Even Jesus, the sinless one, said, "Why do you call Me good? No one is good except God alone" (Mark 10:18). He meant that the entirety of His sinless nature came from His Father, the Source of all goodness. How much more must this apply to us, the inheritors of Adam's defilement? Nothing good originates in me. Whatever I have must flow from Him.

Structures of sin have a life of their own. They function like habits that replay themselves over and over again just beneath the level of our awareness, wounding others and our Lord in spite of our conscious good intentions. The dark night exposes these things and then breaks them through suffering. Jesus forgave our sin on the cross, but that does not automatically dismantle strongholds. We must therefore "pursue . . . the sanctification without which no one will see the Lord" (Hebrews 12:14). The outcome of that pursuit is a cleaner and fuller revelation of the nature of God.

Purpose #3: Abandonment and Despair of Self

The third purpose of the dark night is to bring *complete and total abandonment and despair of self*. If breaking structures of sin opens up a greater revelation of the true nature of God, then it also sharpens my sense of who I really am and of who I am not. On the one hand, I see who I really am in my total depravity, but on the other, because of the revelation of my depravity, I finally see the incredible depth of grace and love in the heart of my God as He covers it, forgives it and chooses me as His servant in spite of it. No prophet can prophesy the pure word without a clear revelation of the Father's love, and no human being can understand the Father's love apart from knowing how much He forgave and what it cost Him to do it.

The foundation of my security can never be in my own performance. Paradoxically, I can be fully secure only when I have finally realized the depth of my personal moral bankruptcy. When I have seen the true depth of my sin, no accusation leveled at me can have any real force. I become unassailably secure because not only am I ready to admit my failure, but I am also at rest in the fullness of the grace and forgiveness I have received. We can never enjoy full freedom without a complete revelation of how imprisoned we have been. Romans 8:1 says, "Therefore there is now no condemnation for those who are in Christ Jesus." In that state there is nothing left to threaten. I can rest in Him only when I have despaired of me. The pure prophetic voice can flow through no other channel than one broken in this way.

Purpose #4: Faith without Agenda

The fourth function of the dark night of the soul is *to bring about faith without agenda or demand of God* by shattering every dream and crucifying every hope. At this writing no prophecy ever spoken over my own life has come to anything like full fruition—and some of those prophecies were the stuff of my dreams, the reasons I "signed on" in the beginning. Would I serve Him and trust Him if my dreams all failed and no word of prophecy spoken over me to set the course of my life ever came to pass? Or is it somehow conditional, as if there were some unspoken contract between two parties, God and me, that binds us both to perform? And if God seems not to carry out His part of the agreement, am I released from mine?

In short, will I die to my agenda in order to be alive to His? Will I trust and obey in faith even when I have been granted not an inkling of what His agenda might be? How long would I be willing to walk blind where the unfolding of destiny is concerned? Will I trust Him enough to die to the dreams and hopes I have lived for all these years?

Or is it somehow all conditional, like that contract? Is God blessing me only when things go well and my prayers are being answered, or will I have the faith to trust that He equally blesses me when the world as I know it comes crashing down around my ears? Will I accept that mystery? I personally am not there yet. Are you? Maybe this is one reason why prophetic ministry in our day is not nearly what it could be. And perhaps this is why some of us have a fair bit more suffering to live through. Only remember that this is training, not punishment. You cannot be on the team and play the game if you will not run the laps in practice. Game time is near and I, for one, intend to be ready.

Purpose #5: Rest for the Higher Functions of the Spirit

The higher functions of the Spirit include ease of movement in the Holy Spirit, hearing God's voice, enjoying real and living fellowship with Him, perceiving Him as He is, Jesus shining in and through us, and so on. In our unbroken and immature state, these functions suffer from the taint of our personal agendas, needs and desires—the ways in which we attempt to manipulate by methods and means in order to obtain what we ourselves feel we must have. One major root of manipulation is unbelief that God will freely honor His promise to provide what we really need. Pure hearing comes only through faith when personal agendas and needs have been set aside. There is a difference between faith *that* God will do a particular thing and faith *in* who God is regardless of what He does. The prophet must walk rested in who God is. The fifth function of the dark night of the soul is therefore *to bring to rest the higher functions of the Spirit.*

Purpose #6: Love for God

The sixth purpose for the long dark night of the soul is *to bring about a love for God that passes beyond loving Him for what He has done or will do for us.* We must love God beyond loving Him for the reward we get from feeling it. As the old song says, "Love is a many splendored thing!" But when it does not feel that way, what then? Would I, Loren Sandford, continue to love Him if it no longer felt good to do it? Could I love Him merely for His own sake apart from the perceived reward of that good feeling for loving Him? The dark night of the soul brings the end of "I love You, Lord, because . . . " It teaches us a deeper love for God when the reward system has been nullified, when we have been deprived of the perception of His touch and the sense of His presence. The psalmist in Psalm 88 reached out in love morning by morning, day by day, even under the burden of what he felt to be utter abandonment by the Object of his love.

Purpose #7: Purity of Fellowship with Him

Just one quote says it all: "That I may know Him and the power of His resurrection and the fellowship of His sufferings" (Philippians 3:10). Paul certainly referred to the physical sufferings he endured under persecution, but he also wrote of another form of suffering. In verses 8 and 9 he said that he had suffered the loss of everything that was his pride and identity in order to gain Jesus. He wrote of the surrender of any sense of personal righteousness. In just a few words he addressed all the issues the dark night of the soul serves to break. The result is *cleaner and purer fellowship with Jesus,* which is the fountainhead of all that is truly prophetic.

Purpose #8: Humility

The dark night of the soul teaches *humility,* and humility forms the basis for the defeat of defensiveness. This flows from security in Jesus, and it leads to transparency and vulnerability. In humility we understand our failings and limitations, but more importantly, with nothing to defend we are much more free to allow failings and weaknesses to show. We no longer need to protect or conceal those tender places inside by putting up a false front of strength that becomes intimidating to the people we have been called to serve. We want to love them, not alienate them. In humble vulnerability they sense that we are truly with them, something absolutely crucial to the ministry of the prophet.

I may be different. I may be set apart. But I am very much one with the people I have been sent to serve. I am connected to them, and they must sense and know the truth of it. Additionally, there is a personal benefit. When you have nothing to hide, people are less likely to use your hidden sin against you. Freedom, both for me and for the people to whom the Lord has sent me, comes when I am no longer the slave of my own self-image.

Purpose #9: Radical Compassion

Compassion flows when I fully and truly identify with sinners. As the perfect One, Jesus identified with us, absorbing our sin and carrying it to the cross to pay the price for it in our place. I must be His disciple, and Scripture teaches, "It is enough for the disciple that he become like his teacher" (Matthew 10:25). I must do it in humility as one who has faced and accepted the magnitude of his own failures. The dark night brings about *cross-centered, compelling compassion.*

Conclusion

At this writing I have spent 47 of my 54 years in and around what history calls the "charismatic renewal." For most of that time we have immersed ourselves in a preoccupation with the gifts of the Spirit—and if not the gifts of the Spirit, then personal blessing, healing and self-improvement. Rather than the Kingdom of God and the welfare of others, self-focus has been the dominant motivating factor.

Many of us have used our spiritual gifts as platforms on which to construct the mansions of our personal ambitions as we have longed for a sense of self-significance. The exercise of spiritual gifts seemed to provide a biblically approved means of satisfying that longing. This is the main reason we see so many prophetic "wannabes" in the Body of Christ these days. Being regarded as prophetic appeals to us as a means of obtaining a sense of recognition and importance. For the longest time it seemed the Father allowed us to get away with it. One does that with children. A good parent makes allowances for immaturity and the foolishness of youth. Up to a point, grace does cover a multitude of sins.

The problem, as I stated earlier, is that the gifts were never ours to begin with. They are His. That is why they are the gifts "of the Spirit." They are not about us. They are about Jesus and His nature. The gifts are tools for delivering the mercy and compassion of Jesus, not platforms for self-realization. I have met supposed prophetic people who said they were looking for a place to "develop" their gift. This is ownership. The Spirit's gifts are not "developed" because He Himself is not "developed." It is we who need developing. The gifts themselves are a finished product.

The heart of prophetic training, therefore, has little to do with learning about dreams, visions and methods of hearing God. Rather, it has everything to do with character development, brokenness and humility. Intimacy with God is the goal. The sin nature and its practices constitute obstacles to achieving that goal. Without the crushing and breaking of the sinful practices and structures of the flesh brought about by the wilderness and the dark night, otherwise good words can and do produce decidedly bad fruit. Good water pumped through a dirty pipe exits the water tap colored by the condition of the pipe.

I know of a few individuals with powerful gifts of discernment and a wide-open spiritual awareness who many think are prophetic, but there is a taint in the anointing—a kind of undertaste that builds up over time as you absorb more and more of their ministry. Gradually under the ministry of one of these you feel invaded, defiled and controlled. A sense of revulsion develops until you want to cut that one off completely. Underneath the apparently gifted exterior is a dominant unbroken need for power—a yearning to be seen and recognized as important, wise and gifted. Such a waste of good raw material! Character is everything. The prophet must be dead to self and alive to God. Make certain you are not one of those whose inner life is so invested in denying your rejection issues that to admit the depth and extent of your depravity would be too much to absorb. Jezebel finds such people an easy mark.

I wish we could crucify ourselves. It might be easier to absorb the pain if this were possible. That would, however, be control. The essence of our training must be loss of control and surrender to the hand of God, even in suffering. So do you still want to be prophetic?

When all has been stripped away, what remains? What value is there in standing naked and broken before God? The answer is the inestimable value of knowing to the core of myself that I am a son, that I am loved and that He is my Father. This is my whole identity. Am I a prophet, a healer, a leader? Recognized or ignored? Well-known or laboring in obscurity? These things no longer matter. What remains is that I am His, secure in His arms. Nothing more. And should that not be enough?

I must reiterate that a new generation of leadership is soon to emerge. Prophetic people will be the forerunners. This leadership will both understand and minister from a base in the Sabbath rest of the people of God:

> So there remains a Sabbath rest for the people of God. For the one who has entered His rest has himself also rested from his works, as God did from His. Therefore let us be diligent to enter that rest, so that no one will fall, through following the same example of disobedience. For the word of God is living and active and sharper than any two-edged sword, and piercing as far as the division of soul and spirit, of both joints and marrow, and able to judge the thoughts and intentions of the heart.
>
> Hebrews 4:9–12

The key in this ministry will be that we will have rested from our own works because we have suffered exposure of every thought and intention of the heart that does not resonate that rest. The flesh avails nothing.

The new leadership is being refined in the crucible of brokenness, the wilderness and the dark night of the soul.

They labor in hiddenness under limitation, learning the sweet simplicity of being nothing more than sons and daughters, but they must soon be revealed and released. In brokenness and humility, walking in the depth of His love, this new generation will be safe to wield the power of God because those elements of flesh that would have abused the flock or usurped the glory of God for self will have been crucified with Christ. This must be the goal, not building great ministries or expanding our influence.

I once heard Bob Jones say, "Five or five thousand, it all pays the same." Until it no longer matters to us where, how or to how many we minister, we are not yet prepared to be prophetic voices in the Kingdom of God.

12

ISSUES OF PLACEMENT IN THE CHURCH

The Church has always contained those who claim to have discovered the definitive form for government and order in the assembly of believers. A specific subset under this would be the roles of prophetic people in worship services and in the wider structure of the Church. Someone always claims to know exactly how the role of the prophetic person should work according to Scripture. Such a large number of variants exists that it would be difficult, if not impossible, to treat them all in the context of this chapter. I therefore offer a summary of what I believe to be right and proper in the context in which I minister. I do not pretend to have the final word or to have discovered the authoritative answer. Scripture leaves room for a variety of practical approaches based on the same set of principles. Substance and spirit are more important than specific forms.

A Three-Pronged Diet

The Jerusalem Church in the days immediately following Pentecost enjoyed a three-pronged diet of meetings (see Acts 2:42–47). They worshiped in the Jerusalem Temple in a large group setting where the awe and power of large numbers of people, artfully orchestrated worship and God-inspired architecture could affect them in marvelous ways. Meetings like this serve to communicate the overall plan of God, reminding us that we are part of something much larger than ourselves and our small circle and inspiring us to be involved in it. The large congregational worship service in most of our churches today would or should be the rough equivalent of this Temple experience in the early Church.

The second prong involved meetings in homes as the believers broke bread from house to house. The Kingdom of God demands real fellowship. It was therefore not enough to have received Jesus; love had to have a place to grow. Covenant relationships needed to be developed. Individual believers needed to learn to walk in the gifts of the Spirit in ministry to one another—and ultimately to the world—in a safe environment. In addition, the Scripture tells us that they devoted themselves to prayer. Where better to pray together than in a home?

The apostles' teaching comprised the third prong. In the earliest days before persecution put an end to it, this was probably done in the porticos of the Temple, where rabbis were free to gather crowds to hear their instruction.

On a regular basis, therefore, the early Church enjoyed large group worship experiences in the Temple, small group fellowship/ministry experiences in homes and the apostles' teaching. This pattern was modified only when persecution denied the Christians in Jerusalem the use of the Temple (it was finally destroyed in AD 70) and when the Gospel moved into regions where larger meeting facilities were unavailable. At that point all three functions had to be consolidated into the only facilities available—people's homes. This home setting forms the context of 1 Corinthians 12 and 14 where the apostle Paul outlined what should happen—and not happen—in a worship service. The pagans had temples. The Christians did not and therefore met in homes.

As the Church grew in power and prosperity in the Roman Empire and was permitted to build large meeting facilities, the center of congregational life gravitated back toward the Temple experience with its awe and grandeur. It should have reverted to the balanced three-pronged approach of the Church in Jerusalem but failed to do so, which launched centuries of sterile Temple-only Christian life without the benefit of the life-giving home group experience where every believer would have an opportunity to contribute. The modern Church ought to recover that balanced approach.

Where do prophetic people fit into all this? How ought they to be placed in the Body of Christ? I submit my personal opinion in the form of practical advice. Again, I do not pretend to have the final and definitive word, but if my understanding and experience can help others, I will be a happy man.

Platforms and Authority

In the large meeting—the Temple experience—the platform is a place of authority and impact on others that is disproportionate to the natures and personalities of those who minister from it. It is as though every word passes through a magnifier that expands and intensifies its impact. When a pastor hands the microphone to another, he has passed both authority and the potential for disproportionate impact to the one who receives it. Any word spoken from the platform in a large meeting carries enormous power to edify or to devastate, to cleanse or to defile. For this reason we must reserve access to the platform for those who have been proven trustworthy and for those who demonstrate respect for the disciplines that may be imposed by leadership.

By contrast, the home setting provides a place where anyone can and should speak without the burden or the impact of magnified authority. The true word stands on its own to edify the group while the false falls to the ground. The gathered group can ignore, forgive or correct error in love. Because of the balance of the fellowship and the covenant relationships that exist in the smaller setting, words can be challenged, weighed and sorted out. The effect of a word spoken in the home group is therefore not the same as the impact of a word spoken in the open assembly.

We must therefore differentiate between those who are merely prophetic and those who hold the office of prophet—or who are at least consistently prophetic—and we must limit access to the platform in the "Temple" meeting to the latter. Home groups are the proper venue for experimenting, weighing and testing words delivered by beginners and by prophetic people who do not hold the office. Paul instructed, "Let two or three prophets speak, and let the others pass judgment" (1 Corinthians 14:29). Clearly this fits best in the relational atmosphere of the kind of home meeting the Corinthians would have held.

Approaches

In thirty years of full-time professional ministry I have approached prophetic ministry in the "Temple" setting in many ways. In the early 1980s I allowed open access to any who felt moved to stand and "prophesy" in the large congregational meeting. Quite honestly, 99 percent of what came forth was vapid sentimentality that merely took up air space, inflated the speaker's own sense of importance and edified no one. I am convinced that God longs to inspire us, not bore us to death. The other 1 percent was mostly harmful condemnation delivered by people looking for a platform from which to vent the spleen of their personal judgments. To be fair, there was one older woman, long steeped in the things of God, who prophesied with depth and humility, but she was the exception to the rule. I no longer allow that kind of free access to the microphone in the large Sunday morning meeting.

I tried requiring prophetic words to be cleared first with a staff member so that we could screen out the bad and make room for the good. Too often I found that what took two sentences to express to a staff member grew limbs and leaves in the actual delivery until it consumed ten agonizing minutes on the platform—and the content turned out to be not much better than before we instituted the screening procedure.

An alternative might be to establish what we called a "word group" back in the 1970s–80s during the heyday of the Charismatic Renewal. This is essentially a group of trusted prophetic people who sit in a designated area of the sanctuary. Any word arising from them can be spoken freely from the platform. Unfortunately in our setting this created an elite group that became visible in its separateness. Divisions resulted.

A solution for pastors who love the gifts and long to see the Spirit move in freedom is to cultivate reliable and consistent prophetic people who share the established vision of the church and work to support it. This can take time.

After thirteen years in my current congregation, I have seen a generation or two of supposed prophetic people come and go and am only beginning to see which ones have remained and passed the tests I have outlined in this book. A few have emerged whom I trust to deliver only edifying messages of real substance in the fewest words possible. I know them to be correctable when shown to be wrong. When one of them sends me the signal during the course of a meeting or gives me a short synopsis of what he or she hears the Lord saying during a time of altar ministry, I happily hand over the microphone, but the days of free access to the platform are over.

Testing

We test for reliability and character in several ways. First, every prophetic person needs to be involved in a small fellowship group that meets regularly in a home. Given all that I have written so far, I will not bore the reader by repeating the reasons why. The home group is the primary place for gifts to emerge and be practiced in the safety and in the checks and balances of covenant relationship. It need not be a group with a prophetic emphasis—it is better if it is not—but it does need to be relational, ministering and studying the Word of God faithfully for the sake of objective grounding in eternal and unchanging truth.

Second, in the belief that prophetic insight is especially valuable in intercessory prayer settings, we test our prophetic people in that environment. Our prayer groups serve many of the same functions as home fellowships but with a specific focus. As we listen for guidance from the Lord and for revelation concerning what God is doing and wants done in prayer, prophetic people quickly emerge and we learn who is reliable, humble and broken. Prophetic insight, humbly expressed, can set the direction of a meeting, gathering all hearts as if in a collective sigh of agreement that says, "Yes!" On the other hand, immature prophetic people, or those with unresolved issues of rejection and need for recognition, often attempt to dominate the meeting. The test then becomes one of correctability and humility.

Third, I invite any who have had "God dreams" or who believe they have received prophetic insight for our church to put these things in writing and submit them to me as pastor. This provides a means of growth for those who have not yet become relationally functional or courageous enough to risk exposing their insights and dreams in an open group setting. It gives me time to weigh their words at my leisure, to speak wisdom into them and encourage or discourage as the case may require. It also provides opportunity to instruct and train in various aspects of interpretation. Occasionally we review dreams in a group setting such as an intercessory meeting where the insights of more than one can be heard and weighed, and where all can learn by participating in the process of interpretation.

Fourth, our church places a high value on ministry teams composed of trained and sensitive laypeople. An average worship service at New Song Fellowship ends with fifteen to twenty ministry team members praying for dozens of people who come forward while others simply linger in worship. We pray for healing, life situations, spiritual breakthrough and anything else that comes up, but we also allow for prophetic ministry one on one. Again, we limit prophetic ministry to those who have demonstrated a degree of maturity and reliability, and we add some rules that basically boil down to: "No direction, correction, dates, mates or babies." Additionally, we have soaking prayer teams that minister an hour at a time by appointment in which team members are free to prophesy but where prophecy is not the main emphasis.

Correction comes in many forms—first from pastoral oversight but also from the Body of Christ itself. We encourage our prophetic people to submit to the correction that comes in the form of reactions from those to whom they minister. No fair taking offense when someone reacts negatively! No fair making excuses for error or for an offensive delivery! Even if the correction is 90 percent wrong, we must be humble enough to receive and take to heart the 10 percent that has substance. Failure itself is a form of correction. Earlier I wrote about journaling. Prophetic people would do well to institute that form of self-correction and be honest with themselves about it when reviewing past entries.

Although many have opened schools for prophets, I question the wisdom of training prophetic people in isolation from the rest of the Body of Christ. Most prophetic people are inherently unbalanced personalities in need of normal people to keep them centered. Put a group of them together in isolation for too long a time and you are begging for insanity. Any school of the prophets should therefore be connected with a healthy and well-balanced congregation filled with normal people to whose welfare the prophetic ministry is dedicated and from whom correction can be received.

Pastoral Oversight

Imbalances and abuses have led many pastors to distance themselves from self-styled prophets who come to them in arrogance rather than with a humble and submitted heart. As a result, too many of us have simply thrown the proverbial baby out with the bathwater. Yes, we should distance ourselves from abusers and from those who come to us presenting their "prophetic résumés" while they reek of pride, ambition and the need for position. I am personally not well liked by quite a number of such people to whom I could not grant the position and recognition they so craved. I cannot give what is not mine to give.

But somewhere in the congregation, often quietly hidden away, God has positioned the real thing. They see things we do not. We need their input, and we must pray for the Holy Spirit to reveal them. We must watch and listen for them. With few exceptions—and I do allow for exceptions—they probably will not be the ones making the most noise. Opening up a venue for sharing dreams can smoke some of them out. In intercessory prayer times, ask those gathered for prayer what they see, feel and sense. Prophetic people will surface in the group as you help them overcome what for many of them is inherent shyness. Draw them forth. Holding or attending a prophetic seminar with a well-known prophetic person can help to identify your prophetic people, as long as care is taken for follow-up.

Once these have been identified, they need pastoring. Draw them close. Listen to them. Filter, correct and balance what they hear. Be part of the reality check they so desperately need. Point out the portions of what they think they hear that fail to square with the eternal Word of God. This is part of fulfilling the instruction in 1 Corinthians 14:29 to pass judgment on prophetic words. As you do this, grant grace for their eccentricities. Don't be put off.

Help them learn to express themselves in ways that can be heard and received by others as edifying. Proverbs 15:2 says, "The tongue of the wise makes knowledge acceptable, but the mouth of fools spouts folly." A true pastor helps his people learn wisdom. Teach them to communicate. Many of them have little or no concept of how others perceive their style of communication. You would train people for effectiveness in any other ministry of the church. Train these! Help them with the inner healing that prophetic people so desperately need. They are worth the investment of your time in counseling. If you cannot be a counseling pastor, then make the effort to connect them with resources that can help. Above all, refuse to be offended or frightened by them.

As opportunity presents itself, help beginners learn the difference between adrenaline flow and true anointing. Many immature prophetic people believe that when their hearts pound and their respiration rates go up, the anointing of the Lord is upon them. These are manifestations of the flesh, not the Spirit. The true word comes with a sense of rest and peace, even if unhealed insecurity causes nervousness in the delivery. Help beginners to discern the difference. Do not just throw them away or discount them for their foolishness.

Misplaced Emphasis

Pastors, either newly enthused by the release of prophetic ministry or too absorbed in it themselves, often err by identifying their churches as prophetic in emphasis. This runs aground on several shoals that have the potential to sink the ship.

First, the New Testament presents a balanced picture of the functioning of the Body of Christ in which the Holy Spirit distributes all His gifts and manifestations "for the common good" (1 Corinthians 12:7). Prophetic ministry has its place, but so do healing, helps, administration, teaching, evangelism and all the rest of the list in order that the Church might value and feed all its members.

In the 1980s, for instance, people tried to identify the church I pastored at the time as a "hospital," or healing, congregation. It sounded good, but we nearly died of it. With that unbalanced emphasis in place, you had to be sick to belong. If you got well, you no longer fit in and needed either to find another problem to be healed or leave. Healthy people felt uncomfortable with us. A similar dynamic takes hold when a church identifies itself as prophetic or places too great an emphasis on prophetic ministry at the expense of other gifts. The many who cannot identify themselves as prophetic soon feel displaced and undervalued. Worse, many who long to belong begin to fancy themselves prophets in order to fit in. This results in rampant pride, delusion, chaos and death. Most of the churches I have known through the years that have identified themselves as having a primary prophetic calling no longer exist. As Mr. Miyagi said to young Daniel in *The Karate Kid*, "Balance, Daniel San! Must learn balance!"

My current congregation fell into this trap for a short time a few years ago. The longer I allowed us to identify ourselves as a prophetic people, the more complaints we heard from people who felt they had no role to play because they were not prophetic. Worse, the longer we held that emphasis, the more polluted and inaccurate prophetic ministry became.

For a time we made prophetic ministry teams available. People could make an appointment with a team of three on a designated night for ten minutes of prophetic input. We recorded each session on cassette to give to the one receiving ministry. We did this for the sake of remembering what was said but also so that accountability for accuracy could be enforced. In the beginning such power fell in the sessions that some folks actually crawled out afterward, unable to stand under the anointing. We received glowing reports. Over time, however, it deteriorated to the point that we began receiving complaints concerning the inaccuracy of the ministry and its failure to edify. We closed it down and have not revived it. Since then, we have been engaged in rebuilding our prophetic ministry and in balancing our church.

Good prophecy edifies. When we minister the real thing, people know God has touched them, and a good deposit is left. Bad prophecy, on the other hand, discredits the ministry in ways few other failures can. Build a balanced ministry. Nurture all the gifts, but especially discipline the prophetic. The word is *discipline*, not *exalt* or *emphasize* and certainly not *suppress*. A close eye in oversight and a diligent and loving hand of guidance can preserve the treasure of an invaluable asset. Neglect will either kill it off or allow it to spin off into insanity.

Conclusion

We urge you, brethren, admonish the unruly, encourage the fainthearted, help the weak, be patient with everyone. See that no one repays another with evil for evil, but always seek after that which is good for one another and for all people. Rejoice always; pray without ceasing; in everything give thanks; for this is God's will for you in Christ Jesus. Do not quench the Spirit; do not despise prophetic utterances. But examine everything carefully; hold fast to that which is good; abstain from every form of evil. Now may the God of peace Himself sanctify you entirely; and may your spirit and soul and body be preserved complete, without blame at the coming of our Lord Jesus Christ.

1 Thessalonians 5:14–23

R. Loren Sandford is the oldest of six children born to John and Paula Sandford, widely recognized as pioneers in the charismatic renewal, prophetic ministry and inner healing. Following a career as a traveling rock musician during his high school years in northern Idaho, Loren attended Albertson College of Idaho in Caldwell, Idaho, where he earned a bachelor's degree in music education in 1973. At college in 1972 he met and married his wife, Beth.

Following graduation they moved to Pasadena, California, where Loren attended Fuller Theological Seminary, earning a master of divinity degree in 1976. While there, Loren and Beth served as youth pastors in a Methodist church in La Palma, California, and brought the first two of their three children into the world. Upon graduation Loren accepted a position as youth pastor at Hope United Methodist Church in Sacramento, where he served for two and a half years.

In January 1979 Loren accepted the invitation to become codirector of Elijah House in Coeur d'Alene, Idaho, alongside his father, who had founded the ministry several years prior. In that position he helped craft the teachings that later became the Elijah House counseling schools while he did personal counseling and pursued an international teaching ministry.

In August 1980 he felt led to plant Cornerstone Christian Fellowship in Post Falls, Idaho, just six miles from the offices of Elijah House. Since Loren's family heritage had been in the Congregational Church (later to become the United Church of Christ), where his father pastored for twenty years before founding Elijah House, it seemed natural to seek ordination in that historic liberal denomination and to work for renewal from within. Cornerstone Christian Fellowship came into existence, therefore, as a member congregation in the United Church of Christ. Loren later served on the national board of directors for Focus Renewal Ministries, the organization working for charismatic renewal within the UCC, as well as continuing to serve as a board member and teacher with Elijah House.

By 1988 the membership of Cornerstone voted to withdraw from the denomination, citing foundational doctrinal differences, and within a few months had found a home with the Association of Vineyard Churches. Three years later Loren accepted a call to become the executive pastor of the Denver Vineyard, then one of the largest Vineyard churches in the nation.

Through a series of confirming circumstances and events, it became clear that Loren was once again to plant a church. In October 1992, New Song Fellowship was born on the north side of the Denver metroplex, where Loren continues as senior pastor.

In 1996, having been profoundly impacted by the Toronto Blessing, New Song affiliated with Partners in Harvest, the network of churches born out of that revival stream. Since then Loren has often served on the international advisory council for Partners in Harvest. In Denver he serves on the steering committee for Denver Metro Transformation, an organization working for Christian unity and community transformation across the metro area. Over the years he has served on many committees working for unity among

Christians, including Rocky Mountain Awake and the March for Jesus.

In Denver Loren has written, produced and recorded eleven music CDs and has authored several books, including *Purifying the Prophetic: Breaking Free from the Spirit of Self-Fulfillment*. From earliest childhood he has been immersed in the move of the Holy Spirit and prophetic ministry. His books reflect a lifetime of experience, gifting and study in the area of prophetic gifting.

He and Beth, married 35 years as of 2007, have two daughters and one son, who have collectively given them seven grandchildren. Loren is also a member of the Osage Nation, a Native American heritage he deeply treasures.

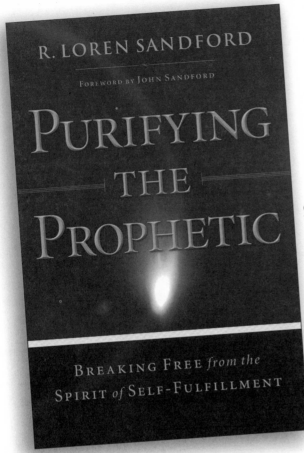